AF326764

THE EVE OF WORLD SOCIALIST REVOLUTION

GERALD McISAAC

Printed in the United States of America

ISBN 978-1-959483-88-5 (sc)
ISBN 978-1-959483-87-8 (hc)
ISBN 978-1-959483-86-1 (e)

Library of Congress Control Number: 2023944965

History
2024.07.14

TABLE OF CONTENTS

INTRODUCTION

On November 7, 1917, new style calendar, the first Soviet Socialist Republic was born, in the republic of Russia. This came about as the result of a revolution, by the workers and peasants of Russia. This revolution was successful because it was led by a truly *Scientific Socialist Marxist*, Political Party, the Bolshevik Party, with Lenin at their head. It was only later that the Party changed its name to that of Communist.

At first, it was not at all clear that the revolution would succeed. It was not until March of 1918, that the Soviets were able to conclude peace with Germany and the Central Powers, and that peace came at a very high price. Russia lost half of their industry, a third of their population, ninety percent of their coal mines, and was forced to pay three hundred million gold rubles.

This was soon followed by a three-year Civil War. The Counter Revolutionaries, or Whites, as they were commonly called, were supported by the British and French, who provided them with the latest military equipment.

At one point, three quarters of the country of Russia was occupied by the Whites. No capitalist country could have withstood the assault. Yet the Bolsheviks, true Marxists, were able to unite the workers and poor peasants, in their opposition to the attack of the invading capitalists. It was not until 1921 that all of the invaders were repulsed. That same year, a peace treaty with Poland was finally signed.

Up until that time, with the war raging, Lenin was focused mainly upon repulsing the invaders. It was only after the enemy forces had been beaten, that he was able to direct his attention to building a socialist society.

Lenin had to face the fact that Russia was one hundred years *behind* America! This is to say that Russia, in 1921, was at the same stage of industrial development as was America, at the time of Jefferson! He also faced the fact that the neighboring capitalist countries are not about to live in peace, with a socialist country! It was just a matter of time before they "came to their senses", quit fighting each other, and focused on destroying the Russian Soviet Socialist Republic.

For that reason, Lenin determined that Russia had to become just as industrialized as America, but that it would do so in *ten years!* He was determined to do in ten years, that which it had taken the American capitalists, *one hundred years* to accomplish! There was no other way to avoid defeat!

For that reason, he started the New Economic Policy. It was a "retreat" from socialism, and he faced strong opposition, even within his own Party. But then, there are times, in war, when it is necessary to retreat, in order to prepare for a fresh offensive. This was one of those times.

Yet Lenin had been shot in 1918. Even though the wounds were not immediately fatal, they led to "complications". He died as a result of those wounds, in 1924.

The policies which Lenin had initiated, were carried through by his successor, Josef Stalin. The country soon developed electricity, and became highly industrialized, through a series of Five Year Plans. Planned production! In this way, they were prepared for the Nazi invasion of 1941.

Truly, Stalin was a great revolutionary. This in no way changes the fact that Stalin made several serious mistakes. As a result of those mistakes, the capitalists were able to return to power, after his death, in 1953.

It is to the credit of the Chinese Communist Party, under Mao Tse Tung, that a proper criticism of Stalin was conducted. They concluded that Stalin was a great revolutionary, but made several mistakes. His mistakes were documented, so that we can learn from those mistakes.

It is also a fact that after the death of Mao, in 1976, the Chinese capitalists were also able to return to power. Without doubt, Mao was also a great revolutionary, but he too made mistakes. As a result of those mistakes, the Chinese capitalists were also able to return to power, after his death.

In a previous article, I have documented at least one of those mistakes, and have suggested a possible correction. There is no need to repeat it here.

This brings us to our current situation, which is similar to the situation which existed at the time of the Russian Revolution of 1917.

At that time, as now, the revolutionary motion was raging, in the most highly industrialized countries of the world. The fact that the revolution failed to spread around the world, is mainly due to a lack of proper leadership. Most of the political parties, which claimed to be Marxist, were chauvinists, Marxist in words, chauvinists in deeds. That is just as true today, as it was in 1917.

This is to stress the importance of a *true* Communist Party, one which is based upon the *revolutionary scientific* theories of Marx and Lenin. Not the least of these scientific theories, in fact the "touchstone" of a true Marxist, is the fact that the existing state apparatus, which has been set up by the capitalists, with the express purpose of crushing the working class, must be abolished. In turn, it must be replaced with a new state apparatus, with the express purpose of crushing the monopoly capitalists, the bourgeoisie, under the Dictatorship of the Proletariat.

Now it is up to those who are aware of the revolutionary scientific theories of Marx and Lenin, mainly middle class intellectuals, to create a true Communist Party, in each of these countries. After all, with few exceptions, it is only such middle class people who are aware of those theories.

No doubt, the revolutionary motion will give rise to revolution in most of the industrialized countries of the world, as well as a number of countries that are not terribly industrialized. It remains to be seen if it gives rise to socialist republics, or merely more capitalist countries, with a different set of rulers.

With the proper leadership, in the form of a true Communist Party, we can expect the existing state apparatus to be smashed, at the time of the revolution. We can further expect a new, working class state apparatus to be established. That new state apparatus is referred to as the Dictatorship of the Proletariat. This new state apparatus is required, in order to crush the monopoly capitalists, the bourgeoisie, as they make every effort to restore their "paradise lost".

Without doubt, the "proper motivation", to establish a true Communist Party, within each country, is coming from the monopoly capitalists, the bourgeoisie. They have just made it clear that they are determined to wipe out the middle class, those who are "Too Small to Succeed".

Equally without doubt, each newly created Communist Party, Dictatorship of the Proletariat, CP, DP, within each country, will lead the forthcoming revolution to true scientific socialism.

At that point, each newly created Independent Socialist Republic, will come together with other Socialist Republics, to form a Union of Independent Socialist Republics, possibly on a world wide scale.

It remains to be seen, if all of those Socialist Republics will give rise to Soviets. Such Soviets, or Councils, are a spontaneous working class creation, a product of revolutionary motion. Yet that same revolutionary motion may give birth to another kind of working class creation. That remains to be seen.

One thing is certain: We are on the eve of a World Socialist Revolution! This will in turn give birth to a Union of World Socialist Republics!

CHAPTER 1

CHAOS IN THE HOUSE

January 3, 2023. The day the new 118 Congress is to be sworn in. Or not! The first order of business is to elect a new Speaker of the House, strictly a formality. As there are only two mainstream political parties in the country, Democrats and Republicans, it is customary for the Party with the majority of seats in the House, to elect their leader as Speaker. Further, as the Republicans, or the GOP, Grand Old Party, as they refer to themselves, have a majority, then it should be "cut and dried". Not this time!

The GOP is every bit as divided as the Democrats! They need 218 votes to elect a Speaker, but have a "razor thin" majority of only four Members! So if even five of their Members vote against their favoured candidate, which is Kevin McCarthy, then he will not be elected as Speaker. Yet on the first ballot, nineteen GOP Members voted against McCarthy! That automatically gave rise to a second ballot, which gave rise to a similar outcome.

This is considered to be serious, as the House cannot vote on any piece of legislation, until they first elect a Speaker! It is only the Speaker of the House who can swear in the next Congress!

Incidentally, the Senate does not have that problem, as it is the duty of the President of the Senate to swear in the next Senate. As the President of the Senate is the Vice President of the United States, that "base has been covered".

The journalists expected some conflict, within the House, as just before the House took a break, on December 23, there was some friction. Yet no one expected anything like this! "Chaos and confusion"! Some Members of the House are referring to this as a "Gong Show", without exactly using the precise word "Gong". The journalists are referring to it as "going down a black hole"! They suspect that "their opponents smell blood"! At the same time, the journalists are careful not to mention the names of the "opponents", although they suspect that Donald Trump is behind this!

They report that over the Christmas break, and possibly for some considerable time before that, a "core group" of "right flank Republicans", led by conservative members of the ''Freedom Caucus", met frequently "behind closed doors", and promised to change the" House Rules".

No wonder they suspect that Trump is behind this! Perhaps now people are taking seriously the statements he made! In particular, Trump said that if he was charged, then people would see "problems …the likes of which perhaps we've never seen". He was not joking!

Yet this is not terribly surprising, at least not to Marxists. It is safe to say that capitalism is in a state of crisis, or more accurately, in a state of numerous crises! I would go so far as to say that capitalism is in its "death throes"! Marx let everyone know what to expect, in the Communist Manifesto:

"Finally, in times when the class struggle nears the decisive hour, the process of dissolution going on within the ruling class, in fact within the whole range of old society, assumes such a violent, glaring character, that a small section of the ruling class cuts itself adrift, and joins the revolutionary class, the class that holds the future in its hands".

That which is taking place now, in the "Hallowed Halls of the House", is simply part of the "process of dissolution", which is going on "within the ruling class". The politicians are merely the loyal and devoted servants of the capitalists, the billionaires, the bourgeoisie. And these, their most devoted servants, are squabbling among themselves!

Now we can expect a "small section of the ruling class" to "cut itself adrift", and to "join the revolutionary class", which is to say the working class, the proletariat. After all, it is the proletariat that "holds the future in its hands".

We can also expect this "small section" to be supremely class conscious, and to bring this awareness of classes to the working class, the proletariat. After all, only the most intelligent, among the ruling class, are able to see the "writing on the wall", are prepared to "cut themselves adrift", to ''abandon the sinking ship". Make no mistake, capitalism has ''had its day"! The days of capitalism are "numbered"! The vast majority of capitalists will not accept this! They will no doubt "go down with the ship"! Fools! Their choice!

To the former capitalists who choose to join the revolutionary forces, I have something to say: Welcome! Brothers and Sisters! Comrades! Join us in building a better world! The World Revolution is now raging! It will very soon set down in North America! You have a key role to play!

No doubt you have a university education, and are aware of the revolutionary theories of Marx and Lenin. Feel free to share this knowledge with the working people, the proletarians. Stress the fact that at the time of the revolution, the existing state apparatus must be smashed. Otherwise the leaders of the revolution will merely take over that state apparatus, and set themselves up as the new rulers. A new state apparatus must be set up, in order to crush the capitalists, as they try to restore their "paradise lost". This is known as the Dictatorship of the Proletariat.

Feel free to take part in Councils. Now is not the time for false humility! The fact that you have joined the progressive revolutionary forces, proves that you are a leader! We need leaders! Get in touch with the leaders of other Councils, and work towards forming a true Communist Party, Dictatorship of the

Proletariat! Bear in mind that Marx and Lenin were also middle class intellectuals!

As I write this, the Members of the House have voted no less than three times. Each time, a "hard core group" of possibly twenty Republicans have consistently voted against McCarthy. Now the leaders are "meeting behind closed doors", in secret, hidden from the public, the very people they are supposed to be representing!

The journalists are reporting that the last time this happened was in 1923. At that time, no less than nine ballots took place, before a Speaker was elected. Even so, that was far faster than the previous time the House was deadlocked, in the "eighteen fifties" At that time the country was deeply divided, on the verge of Civil War! For that reason, it took 133 votes, over a two-month period, before a Speaker was elected! The country is just as divided now, as it was in the eighteen fifties!

The House has just agreed to shut down until tomorrow. The journalists are reporting the "GOP in Open Revolt", that "All Business Is On Hold". They are even reporting that "some GOP moderates are laying the groundwork to team up with Democrats"!

Truly, this is an indication that we are "near the decisive hour", as "the process of dissolution within the ruling class", has truly assumed a "violent, glaring character". May the protesters now sing the Internationale! May the banners and posters now proclaim:

Revolution!
Scientific Socialism!
Workers of the World, Unite!
Dictatorship of the Proletariat!

CHAPTER 2

MORE CHAOS IN THE HOUSE

Day 2 of the struggle, in the House of Representatives, to elect a Speaker of the House. Until the House elects a Speaker, the House, and almost all of the federal government, is completely paralyzed!

On day one, the Members of the House managed to take three votes, in order to elect a new Speaker. All three votes failed, almost identically. So of course on day 2, they took another three votes, also with an identical result. We cannot help but wonder what they expected!

The journalists are doing a fine job of reporting the fact that the House is "completely paralyzed", that it is "dysfunctional", that this display of incompetence "erodes confidence" in the government, that there is "chaos among the House GOP". All of this is very true!

As a result of this, those same journalists are agreed that the House is facing a "messy two years ahead".

I mention this as an example of the strengths, and weaknesses, of bourgeois journalism. On the one hand, they do a fine job of stating the facts. On the other hand, their analysis, including their "predictions", are frequently in direct contradiction of the facts!

The journalists even go so far as to say that this is "democracy in action". That is true, as far as it goes! They neglect to add that it is *bourgeois democracy!* It is democracy for the *capitalists!* Democracy for the *billionaires!* For the working people, it is a *dictatorship!*

The point must be driven home, to the working class, that democracy is a method of *class rule!* It most certainly is *not* majority rule! As we live under the rule of the monopoly capitalists, the billionaires, technically referred to as the bourgeoisie, it is the rule of the bourgeoisie.

The monopoly capitalists, the billionaires, must be overthrown. That can happen only through revolution! At that point, the existing state apparatus must be smashed, and a new working class state apparatus must be established. That is referred to as the Dictatorship of the Proletariat.

Without doubt, we live in a time of revolution. The suffering of the working people has reached horrendous proportions. Hunger is wide spread. Homelessness is common place, and increasing. Gang violence and multiple homicides are now daily events. Drug overdoses and suicides are routine. Now galloping inflation is merely intensifying the suffering. People can no longer continue to live this way!

Yet that is *not enough!* For a revolution to "triumph", it is also "essential that the exploiters should not be able to live and rule in the old way", as explained by Lenin.

In our case, the "exploiters" are represented by the politicians in the House. That same House is in a state of "gridlock". The Republican Party is now at war with itself. The finest of the bourgeois minds, see "no way forward". In short, the capitalists are now unable to "live and rule in the old way", which is one of the conditions for a successful revolution.

Lenin goes on to say that such a governmental crisis "draws even the most backward masses into politics…weakens the government, and makes it possible for the revolutionaries to rapidly overthrow it".

The significance of the paralysis, within the government, lies in the fact that countless working people have been "drawn into action". The government is now "weakened". Now it is possible to "rapidly overthrow it"!

The working people are listening closely, as the journalists explain that the important decisions are being made "behind closed doors". The cameras show the politicians huddled in groups, plotting and scheming. The working class is receiving an education!

Now it is up to Marxists, true Communists, to raise their level of awareness even higher. The working class must be made aware of itself as a class, with its own class interests. These interests are diametrically opposed to the interests of the capitalists, the billionaires. We must use the events in the House, the "government gridlock", to drive home the correctness of the revolutionary theories of Marx and Lenin.

Incidentally, the fact is that Trump is asking all Republican Members of the House to vote for McCarthy, as Speaker. This means that Trump must consider McCarthy to be "in his pocket". Yet no less that twenty Republican Members of the House are defying Trump! So Trump must be losing his control over the Republican Party!

It is also a fact that, as Lenin stated, a "great revolution", and especially a "socialist revolution", gives rise to "chaos …among all the elements of disintegration of the old society".

This explains the "chaos", which is currently taking place in the House! It is merely one of the "elements of disintegration of the old society"! As the capitalist society is "disintegrating", it is giving rise to "chaos"!

Strangely enough, even though the bourgeois journalists bear witness to this, they either cannot, or perhaps will not, face the fact that the "old society" is in a state of "disintegration". A world without capitalism, a world of socialism, is "on the horizon".

That in no way changes the fact that we can use the facts which the journalists present, to drive home to the working class the necessity for revolution. At the same time, we must stress the necessity of smashing the existing state apparatus, and replacing it with the Dictatorship of the Proletariat. That is the "way forward"!

CHAPTER 3

GOVERNMENT DEFAULT IMMINENT

January 19, 2023. D Day! On that day, according to the Treasury Secretary, the United States will reach the debt ceiling limit. Thirty-one point four *trillion* dollars! That is as far as they can go! By law, the country cannot go any deeper into debt. Unless, of course, the debt ceiling is raised, as President Joe Biden, a Democrat, has in mind. This is generally a mere formality, as it has been raised numerous times in the past. Yet this year is different.

The problem is that the debt ceiling can only be raised by the House of Representatives, which is commonly referred to as the Congress. The Democrats have just lost control of the House, to the Republican Party, also known as the GOP, the Grand Old Party.

The GOP may be divided on a great many issues, but they are united in their opposition to an increase in the debt ceiling.

The Speaker of the House is now Kevin McCarthy, a Republican, who managed to secure that position, but only on the *fifteenth* ballot! The Congress has not been this deeply divided since the days of the Civil War! Not a coincidence!

In order to secure sufficient votes to become Speaker, McCarthy had to make certain concessions, "behind closed doors", to "Right Wing" members of his Party, according to the journalists. Even the other Republican Members of Congress are not aware of the details of these "secret agreements"!

The journalists are reporting that the "rank and file" GOP Members are furious! They are convinced that McCarthy has agreed to "multiple backroom concessions" in order to secure the Office of Speaker of the House.

Their bitterness is understandable! The Members who were the most loyal, devoted and reliable, those who have consistently voted along Party lines, have received no reward! The "vocal minority", those who were labelled as "trouble makers", have won! They are in their glory! They have been promised "Lord knows what"! McCarthy is not saying! Truly, the "squeaky wheel gets the grease"!

The rank and file GOP Members are venting their frustrations to the journalists. They are referring to this as a "conspiracy of silence". They are claiming that McCarthy just "destroyed the Republican Party, as well as the House". In order to secure his position as Speaker, he "systematically destroyed the norms and institutions of democracy". They are referring to this as an "Insurrection by other means".

Without doubt, such wild talk has never been heard before, in the House! At least not in recent memory! McCarthy is even being accused of "institutionalizing the chaos", of "attacking the functioning of government"!

As a result of this, the journalists are speculating that a "government shutdown", and even a *default* on the national debt", is "more likely, if not probable". They are blaming this on McCarthy, for "sacrificing the Congress". As they put it, the "saboteurs have won".

This is not to say that the government will shut down on January 19. Indeed, not! The plan, of the Treasury Secretary, is to "resort to extraordinary measures". Apparently this is a reference to "creative bookkeeping", otherwise known as "robbing Peter to pay Paul".

In a "worst case scenario", she expects the government to default on the national debt by early June. Yet she still has a clear set of priorities. In such a case, she maintains that it is essential to first "make the interest payments on the national debt". After that, the remaining tax revenue can go towards the "military, Social Security, Medicare and Veterans Benefits".

First and foremost, the *interest payments*! Make sure that those who own the banks, get paid first! The owners of these banks are composed of a class of people, referred to as the monopoly capitalists, the billionaires, technically referred to as the bourgeoisie!

The Treasury Secretary is a loyal and devoted servant of the capitalists! Let the hungry stay hungry! Let the homeless stay homeless! The gang violence is not her concern! Drug overdoses are not her concern! Let the infrastructure of the country fall apart! The banks must be paid!

The point of all this is to drive home the point that the "class struggle'" has assumed a "violent, glaring character", so that we are close to the "decisive hour". In other words, socialist revolution, and the Dictatorship of the Proletariat, is "right around the corner"!

Yet this will not happen by itself! At the time of the Great Russian October Revolution of 1917, there existed in Russia a proper Communist Party, one which called for the Dictatorship of the Proletariat. That base was covered! It was the Communist Party which provided the proper leadership. Yet that was not enough.

As Lenin stated, in reference to the Great Russian October Revolution of 1917, that "success depended entirely upon the existence of available organizational forms of a movement embracing millions".

Those "organizational forms", appeared in the form of soviets, or Councils, in English. At the time of the October Socialist

Revolution, the existing state apparatus, of the capitalists, was promptly destroyed, and replaced by the Soviets.

Incidentally, as I have no way of knowing which word will become common place, I have chosen to use the word Soviet, at least for the purposes of this article.

This is to drive home the point that the Soviets are critically important. After the revolution, they will be placed in key positions of authority. They will be part of the Dictatorship of the Proletariat. The current leaders of the existing soviets are well advised to bear that in mind. To such people, I have a bit of advice: *Be prepared!*

The revolution will happen, when it happens! No one knows the spark that will set the country ablaze! We just know that the country is a "powder keg"! We also know that the revolution is raging around the world! It is urgent that the leaders of these soviets prepare for the revolution! Train your people to take part in the insurrection! Raise their level of awareness! Transform them into class conscious Communists! Encourage them to read the revolutionary works of Marx and Lenin! Stress the importance of the Dictatorship of the Proletariat! Use the events in Washington to drive home, to all working people, the necessity of revolution!

At the same time, get in touch with the leaders of other Soviets. Coordinate your actions! Create a true Communist Party, Dictatorship of the Proletariat! The need for this is urgent! Working people need leaders!

Also, get in touch with Soviets in other countries. Use the internet! Remain anonymous, but vocal! Expect them to make every effort to crush the revolution! Watch your back! Arresting the leaders is a time honored tradition! Do not make it easy for the capitalists!

Bear in mind that not all revolutions give rise to Soviets, in all countries. Certain countries may give birth to a new type of power, "proletarian power", according to Lenin. Whatever works! The important thing is that these "organizational forms", are to be used in the forthcoming revolution, and the subsequent Dictatorship of the Proletariat. As the Socialist Revolution is raging around the world, it will soon give rise to that which Lenin foresaw:

A World Socialist Republic!

CHAPTER 4

DEFAULT: A DISTINCT POSSIBILITY

The country has officially reached the "debt ceiling", according to the Treasury Secretary. So now she is resorting to "extraordinary measures" to "stay under the debt limit". Even so, she anticipates the country will "default on the national debt by early June", unless the "debt ceiling is raised".

The federal government is now "on the horns of a dilemma", as two branches of that government, the executive and the legislative, are "at each other's throats".

The executive branch, led by President Biden, a Democrat, is determined to raise the debt ceiling, without cutting social spending. The legislative branch, which is to say the Senate and the House of Representatives, has other ideas. The fact of the matter is that the House controls the money! It is further a fact that the House is now controlled by Republicans!

The journalists are now reporting that a sizeable minority of Republican Members of Congress, possibly "forty or so", are "in control". They have formed something they refer to as a "Freedom Caucus", within the Republican Party, the GOP. The journalists refer to this Caucus as "Ultra Conservative", or "Extreme Right Wing".

It is further the opinion of the journalists, that the House Speaker is now a mere "figure head", a "puppet", that he "dances to their tune", that of the Freedom Caucus. They have a point!

The Republicans have a "razor thin" majority in the House, that of a mere four votes. This gives the members of the Freedom Caucus considerable power, which they are only too anxious to use! In fact, the only way McCarthy could secure enough votes to be elected as Speaker, was to make numerous concessions to the Freedom Caucus. He has been accused of "giving away the House".

One of those concessions is that of allowing any Member, at any time, to demand a vote for a new Speaker. Such a demand will automatically shut down the House, until after a successful vote, in which a Speaker is elected. During the time of the vote, the government is effectively paralyzed. The last time that happened, it required fifteen votes, over a period of several days. That is not something they want to repeat!

The Members of the Freedom Caucus are determined to *not* raise the debt ceiling, or at the very least, agree to raise the debt ceiling, but *only* if it is tied to significant cuts in social spending.

Yet Biden is determined to raise the debt ceiling, without cutting social spending, if only because he is focused on serving a second term. So now he is considering "new and creative" ways to do so, perhaps "bypassing" the Congress. This may also involve violating *the Constitution!*

The closest advisers of Biden are suggesting that he should merely raise the debt ceiling, without the approval of Congress. They maintain that the Fourteenth Amendment to the Constitution gives him the right to declare the debt ceiling to be Unconstitutional!

They have in mind the clause which states "no state shall make or enforce any law which shall abridge the privileges or immunities of the citizens of the Unites States".

Such details, as declaring a law to be Unconstitutional, are generally considered to be under the jurisdiction of the Supreme Court. So say the experts on Constitutional law!

Yet the advisors to President Biden are of a different opinion! They are encouraging him to "take unilateral action", to raise the debt ceiling, without the approval of Congress! They assure him that as President, he has the authority to make that "executive decision". They also assure him that should the Supreme Court object, and rule that such an action is Unconstitutional, then he, as President, could respond by declaring the Supreme Court decision to be "inconsistent with the Constitutional duties of the President", and ignore the ruling of the Supreme Court!

Incredible! Even more incredible, it is not without precedent!

This has happened before, during the Civil War. At that time, President Lincoln suspended the rights of citizens to a "writ of habeas corpus". This is to say that the right of "unlawful and indefinite imprisonment" was suspended, by President Lincoln. He ordered the arrest and imprisonment of countless people, for any reason, or for no reason, and for as long as he saw fit! He maintained that he had the right to do so, under the authority of the "War Act". Further, he did this without Congressional approval!

These actions were brought to the attention of the Supreme Court. It ruled that President Lincoln did not have the right to arrest people and hold them indefinitely!

President Lincoln in turn *defied* this ruling, of the Supreme Court! As he phrased it, "Are all the laws but one to go unexecuted, and the government itself to go to pieces, lest that one be violated?"

This in no way alters the fact that President Lincoln took an oath to "preserve, protect and defend the Constitution", and then broke that very oath!

The advisers to President Biden are telling him to also break his oath! To violate the Constitution! This could well be considered to be nothing less than an *Act of High Treason!*

As for those who think that this could not possibly happen, as the United States is a democratic republic, may I suggest that you face the facts. The fact is that the monopoly capitalists, the billionaires, the bourgeoisie, are members of a class of people who are technically referred to as imperialists. Further, as Lenin stated, quite clearly, "imperialism is reaction, right down the line"!

It is entirely possible that President Biden will stoop to the depth of violating the Constitution. It is even possible that he will use the Fourteenth Amendment to the Constitution, as justification for that violation! That and the fact that President Lincoln has already set the precedent!

The American people are not about to take that lying down! We can expect widespread opposition!

In such a case, we will no doubt be faced with a very strange alliance! We can expect the "Ultra-Right", including the "Freedom Caucus", as well as the "MAGA People", to come together with the "Leftist People", including those who are thought to be "Ultra Left", the "Communists", in opposition to President Biden! Impeach Biden! Remove him from office! This despite the fact that Kamala Harris would automatically become President! Truly, "politics makes for strange bedfellows"!

I should mention that another option, which Biden and his councilors are seriously considering, is to *Mint a Trillion Dollar Coin*"! For that matter, they could mint a score of them, and declare the country to be debt free! They could even have a surplus! (Joking!)

Those are the options, which both Speaker of the House McCarthy, and President Biden, are considering. If McCarthy "gives in" to Biden, then he will be "voted out" as Speaker. On the other hand, if Biden "gives in" to McCarthy, he will be "voted out", at the next election. This is commonly referred to as "being caught between a rock and a hard place"! A government default appears to be ever more likely!

In the Communist Manifesto, Marx and Engels let us know what to expect. This "gong show", within Washington, is nothing other than part of the "process of dissolution", within the old society, during the time in which the "class struggle nears the decisive hour".

As a result of this, we can now expect a "small section of the ruling class to cut itself adrift, and join the revolutionary class, the class that holds the future in its hands".

In our case, that revolutionary class is the proletariat, as it is the proletariat that "hold the future in its hands".

It also means that revolution can break out at any time, as it is clear that we are approaching the "decisive hour". We had best be prepared!

This is to stress the importance of preparing the working class for revolution, and the subsequent Dictatorship of the Proletariat. After the revolution, many workers will be placed in positions of authority! Any training they receive now, will prove to be most valuable! That is much preferable to no training!

At the very minimum, it is up to conscious people, Communists, to make workers aware of themselves as the members of a working class, of proletarians. It is the *duty* of workers to overthrow the capitalists, the billionaires, the bourgeoisie, and crush them, under the Dictatorship of the Proletariat. As I have covered this in previous articles, there is no need to repeat it here. Allow me to merely stress the importance of performing this quickly. That which the capitalists refer to as "X Day", the day on which the government "defaults on the national debt" is fast approaching. That could well trigger a revolution.

CHAPTER 5

APPROACHING FRENCH REVOLUTION

The current revolutionary movement has taken the form of strikes, in a great many industrialized countries of the world. This is most encouraging, an indication that the World Socialist Revolution is on the horizon.

Yet for the purposes of this article, I have chosen to focus on the country of France. There is a reason for this. It was Engels who stated, in his introduction to the third edition of the book by Marx, The Eighteenth Brumaire, that:

''France is the land where, more than anywhere else, the historical class struggles were each time fought out to a decision, and where, consequently, the changing political forms within which they occur and in which their results are summarized have likewise been stamped with the sharpest outlines. The centre of feudalism in the Middle Ages, the model country of centralized monarchy resting on estates since the Renaissance, France has demolished feudalism in the Great Revolution and established the unalloyed rule of the bourgeoisie in a classical purity unequalled by any other European land. And the struggle of the upward striving proletariat against the ruling bourgeoisie also appeared here in an acute form unknown elsewhere''.

Writing several years later, in 1917, Lenin was of the opinion that: "The last sentence is out of date, inasmuch as a lull has occurred in the revolutionary struggle of the French proletariat since 1871; although, long as this lull may be, it does not preclude the possibility that, in the coming proletarian revolution, France may once again reveal itself as the classical land of the class struggle to a conclusion".

Now that the "lull" is over, it is very likely that France will "once again reveal itself as the classical land of the class struggle to a conclusion". The current class struggle is between the monopoly capitalists, the bourgeoisie, and the common people, mainly the proletariat, although there are a considerable number of farmers, referred to as les paisans, as well as a sizeable middle class, la petite bourgeoisie. These "lower classes" are quite well united against the plan of the current French government to raise the retirement age by two years, from sixty-two to sixty-four.

The government of Macron says that the plan to raise the retirement age is "non-negotiable". Yet the French working people are not negotiating. They are taking action.

The trade unions are leading the struggle against the capitalists, with a series of strikes. On January 19, the press reports that all the unions went on strike, so that "all local and national transport across the country was severely disrupted". The journalists estimate that more than one million people took part in demonstrations, on that day alone.

The crowds were especially large in Paris, with a combination of young and old, complete with "singing and dancing, a festive atmosphere, defiant, high morale, some people from far away, all determined to enact change".

Other protests take the form of "Robin Hood operations", in that workers give away free petrol and electricity to schools, universities and low income households. Even some police are reported to be on strike!

The French bakers, those who are mainly la petite bourgeoisie, small business owners, are also on strike. They are being strangled by the high prices of electricity, as well as the prices of flour, sugar, butter and other ingredients.

The CGT Union, Confederation Generale du Travail, which represents transport workers, has called for refinery workers and other staff on the petrol sector to strike for 48 hours, from February 6. Similar strikes in 2022 saw petrol stations run dry and drivers waiting hours to fill up their tanks. As well, mass strikes are being encouraged by French unions on Tuesday, February 7, and Saturday, February 11. The worst "disruption" is anticipated to be on February 7, and could "spill over" into February 8.

The press is also reporting that the SNCF, Societe National des Chemins de Fer Francais, plan strikes on February 7, 8, and 11. The journalists quite helpfully point out that we can expect "train circulation in France to be very disrupted". That is the general idea!

There is a reason that Marxists, true Communists, consider these strikes to be of the utmost importance. In the early stages of capitalism, they start out as the natural result of large scale factory production, in that workers are forced to fight for better wages and working conditions. But as the class struggle approaches the point of revolution, the strikes assume a political character.

This requires a little explanation.

Capitalism is the name of the social system under which we all live, at least for now. This is to say that society is split up into classes. The monopoly capitalists, or billionaires, technically referred to as the bourgeoisie, own almost all the factories, mines, mills, railroads, airlines, banks and communication networks. In fact, they own or control almost everything of any great value. Although few in number, because of their wealth, they have great power.

The rest of the population have very little, some with next to nothing. Those who have nothing are referred to as workers, or proletarians. They are reduced to selling themselves, by the hour, to the capitalists. Of course, these workers always try to secure the highest possible wages.

By contrast, the capitalists are focused on paying their workers as little as possible, in order to achieve the highest possible profit.

To the surprise of absolutely no one, the result is that of conflict, in that the workers are constantly trying to secure higher wages and working conditions, and the capitalists are constantly trying to reduce wages. This is referred to as "class struggle", at least by the social scientists. Most working people simply refer to this as a normal situation: War!

At first, a more advanced worker generally notices that there is strength in numbers. This worker then usually becomes a leader, bringing together as many workers as possible, in order to make demands upon the capitalist. A revolt takes place. The result is then a work stoppage, a strike. Workers then lash out in anger and frustration, as they are not aware of that which they are trying to achieve. They simply smash the machines and destroy the factories.

At that stage, as Lenin phrased it, "They merely want to display their wrath to the factory owners; they are trying out their joint strength in order to get out of an unbearable situation, without yet understanding why their position is so hopeless and what they should strive for".

Yet at some point, cooler heads prevail. They realize that destroying machines and factories may be gratifying, but fails to put money in their pocket. Instead, occupying the factories as a group, or union, and demanding better wages, before returning to work, is the answer. In this way the working class advances.

As Lenin stated, "The slaves begin to put forward the demand to become masters, not to work and live as the landlords and capitalists want them to, but as the working people themselves want to. Strikes, therefore, always install fear into the capitalists, because they begin to undermine their supremacy...The wheel of this machine is set in motion by *the worker*…When the workers refuse to work, the entire machine threatens to stop. Every strike reminds the capitalists that it is the workers and not they who are the real masters…Every strike reminds the workers that their position is not hopeless, that they are not alone." (italics by Lenin)

Even though strikes mean great hardships for the workers, those who take part in the strikes receive great respect from the workers of neighboring factories. They too are inspired, receive renewed courage. Such strikes tend to spread to neighboring factories.

More importantly, according to Lenin, "Every strike brings thoughts of socialism very forcibly to the worker's mind, thoughts of the struggle of the entire working class for emancipation from the oppression of capital."

Remarkably enough, even the capitalists are aware of this! It is with good reason that a certain German minister proclaimed, "Behind every strike lurks the hydra (monster) of revolution"! The capitalists have every reason to be afraid of strikes! We have every reason to use strikes to raise the level of awareness of the working class!

It is up to Marxists, Communists, to get in touch with the people who are protesting, in France. Without doubt, they are discussing socialism. They must be encouraged to become aware of the revolutionary theories of Marx and Lenin. Now that we have the Internet, this is not at all difficult. It just requires people to send them emails, in the French language, of course.

Feel free to remind them of their proud revolutionary history, and not only the Revolution of 1789. Also the Paris Commune of 1871, which established the first Workers Republic. It is very likely that the French government would like to forget about that, especially as the Commune was crushed, by the capitalists, with the utmost brutality. Yet it was the Paris Commune that provided Marx with the information he needed. It displayed the structure of the first Socialist Republic in the world. The heroism and sacrifice of the Communards will never be forgotten! We can only hope that the current French protesters will be inspired by the example of their glorious ancestors! Feel free to honor their memory by following in their footsteps! Establish another Commune, but this time not only in Paris!

Further, the manner in which the Commune was crushed, by the capitalists, should dispel all doubts concerning the attitude of the current French capitalists! They too are butchers! They must be overthrown, their state apparatus must be smashed, and then they must in turn be crushed, by the Dictatorship of the Proletariat! Do not make the mistake of the Paris Communards! Do not be merciful to the capitalists! The Communards made that mistake, and paid for it with their lives! Take the advice of Marx! Learn from the mistakes of the Communards!

We can only hope that the French strikers and protesters will download revolutionary literature from the Internet, such as the Communist Manifesto. I also recommend essential works of Lenin, such as What Is to Be Done? State and Revolution, Imperialism, the Highest Stage of Capitalism, and Left Wing Communism, An Infantile Disorder. Such works may have to be ordered online. Rest assured, they are well worth the money.

Bear in mind that the Paris Commune was crushed, for a number of reasons. The Communards made a few mistakes. Not the least of these mistakes was in *not* following the advice of Marx!

The world is watching. Feel free to honor the memory of your ancestors by following the advice of Marx and Lenin. Walk in the footsteps of your heroic ancestors, and take a step beyond the Paris Commune:

Create a France Commune!

CHAPTER 6

STATE OF THE UNION, 2023: ANARCHY!

President Biden just delivered his annual State of the Union address. It was a peculiar mixture of fantasy and philosophy. Any resemblance to reality was conspicuous by its absence.

His appeal to the opposition Republican Party, the GOP, was a classic example of wishful thinking. As a professional speech writer is responsible for all of the speeches of the president, we can only suggest that Biden fire that incompetent fool. The President merely reads from a teleprompter. That which he read was at best, an embarrassment. At worst, a pack of lies:

"To my Republican friends, if we can work together in the last Congress, there is no reason we can't work together in this new Congress. The people sent us a clear message. Fighting for the sake of fighting, power for the sake of power, conflict for the sake of conflict, gets us nowhere."

Reality check, Mr. President, you do not have any Republican friends! Certainly not in the House of Representatives! You certainly did not work with them in the last Congress! You worked *against* them! The Republicans were in a minority in that Congress, and they fought you tooth and nail! Now they are in a majority, and they are still fighting you! Yet you are right about one thing: you are getting "nowhere"!

This State of the Union address was possibly the only one, at least in recent memory, to be heckled by the Members of Congress! Those Members were openly booing, calling Biden a liar! They have a point!

Biden said that his "vision for the country" is to "restore the soul of the nation, to rebuild the backbone of America, the middle class, to unite the country".

No chance, Mr. President! The "soul of the nation", or the "backbone of America", as you referred to the middle class, has been all but wiped out! The monopoly capitalists have succeeded in driving smallest business owners into the ground! They simply cannot compete with the monopolies! And it is the small business owners who comprise the middle class! That is not about to change! The monopolies are becoming ever bigger, ever stronger!

As for your goal to "unite the country", that is not about to happen! The fact of the matter is that the country is divided into classes. On the one hand, we have a very small minority of monopoly capitalists, billionaires, referred to as the bourgeoisie, and on the other hand we have the vast majority of working people, mainly composed of hourly employees, referred to as the proletariat.

As the capitalists pay their hourly employees as little as possible, in order to achieve the greatest possible profit, and their hourly employees are constantly trying to increase their wages, it is clear that their interests are diametrically opposed. That which is in the best interest of one class, is in the worst interest of the other class. There is no way the two classes, capitalists and workers, are about to unite! They are class enemies!

This class conflict recently came to the surface, within the House of Representatives.

Within the House, there are several Members, all Democrats, who are referred to as "The Squad". They have been labelled as

"Ultra Left", and worse. Possibly all of them have a working class background.

Bear in mind that the expression of "The Squad" is not mine. Yet in my opinion, these Members of the Squad are nothing other than the proletarian headquarters, within the House. It is very likely that they are not aware of this. On the other hand, they recently received a rude awakening, a lesson in class conflict.

One Member of the Squad was just kicked off of her seat on the House Foreign Affairs Committee. There followed a number of emotional, passionate speeches, by the Members of the Squad. One of them, who is widely considered to be the unofficial leader of The Squad, stated that since 911, people of color and Muslim Americans have been targets of racism. She maintains that, even in the House, women of color have been the target of racism and violence.

In all fairness to the capitalists, that is not entirely true. In fact, *all* people of color, including women and Muslim Americans, have been targets of racism and violence, since *long before* 911! In the House and outside the House! The members of The Squad are just now becoming aware of this! Progress!

Her response was quite gratifying. As she put it, "My voice will get louder and stronger and my leadership will be celebrated around the world, as it has been"! Well spoken, young lady! Precisely the sort of thing we need to hear, in Washington and elsewhere! Keep it up!

Now it is up to us, working people, the members of the public, to support her and the other members of The Squad, in every way possible! We can expect them to come under ever more intense pressure! They need our support!

That support includes sending other working class people to Washington, and not just to the capital of the nation. Also to the various state capitals, among other places. Americans can manage this by joining the two mainstream political parties, as card carrying members, and appointing working class candidates to run for office. As I have covered this in a previous article, there is no need to repeat it here.

No doubt, there are a great many people who want nothing to do with the "cesspool of Washington". Such an attitude is completely understandable, but mistaken. It is important to keep the "big picture" in mind.

As Lenin stated, the "main thing" is to "win over" the "vanguard of the proletariat". Without this, "not even the first steps towards victory can be made".

This begs the question: How do we win over the vanguard of the proletariat?

The level of awareness of the most advanced strata of the working class, the proletariat, must be raised to that of the level of conscious people, of Marxists, or Communists, if you will. They have got to be made aware of the existence of classes, and of the conflict between the classes. They must further be made aware of the necessity of revolution, of smashing the existing state apparatus, and setting up another state apparatus, in the form of the Dictatorship of the Proletariat. It is necessary to crush the desperate and determined resistance, of the bourgeoisie, after the revolution, as they try to restore their "paradise lost".

Working people are not impressed by passionate speeches! They are impressed by action! It is up to intellectuals of all persuasions, and not just Communists, to become involved in that which interests the working class, to use these as examples, to explain the class conflict involved, of the necessity of overthrowing the billionaires, which is only possible through revolution, and of the subsequent Dictatorship of the Proletariat. There is no other way of establishing a socialist society!

An example of that which has the attention of the working class, is the State of the Union address. We know this for a fact, because it was aired on prime time! The only reason the capitalists broadcast anything on prime time, is because countless people are expected to watch it!

As that is the case, it is up to us to respect the beliefs of all working people. That includes the beliefs of those who still have faith in the current democratic process! It is clear that many people still follow the lead of such people as Trump and Biden.

For that reason, we must point out the hypocrisy of both mainstream political parties, Democratic and Republican. Both parties serve the same class!

With that in mind, we should participate in all elections, perhaps assisting working people in running for Congress, Senate, Governors of various states, etc. Then, from *within* Washington, assist The Squad, in exposing the government corruption, as those officials are nothing but the loyal and devoted servants of the capitalists.

Working people must learn, from experience, that the capitalists are completely corrupt, are in charge, and fully intend to remain in charge!

Lenin was not joking when he stated, "The proletariat must train its *own* politicians, 'class politicians", of a kind in no way inferior to bourgeois politicians". (italics by Lenin)

After all, the fact is that revolution is impossible without a change in the views of the *majority* of the working class, a change brought about by the political experience of *all* of the common people, never by propaganda alone. Hence the need to send working class people to Washington, to join and support The Squad.

Bear in mind that the "Fundamental Law of Revolution", as per Lenin, is as follows: "For a revolution to take place, it is not enough for the exploited and oppressed masses to realize the impossibility of living in the old way, and demand changes; for a revolution to take place it is essential that the exploiters should not be able to live and rule in the old way. It is only when the *'lower classes' do not want* to live in the old way and the 'upper classes' *cannot carry on in the old way* that the Revolution can triumph". (Italics by Lenin)

Almost all Americans can testify to the fact that it is simply not possible to continue to live, as they are now. Violent crime is common place, with mass shootings, on a regular basis. Drug overdoses are epidemic. Hunger is a constant companion. Food banks are running out of food. The number of homeless is growing daily. Inflation is sky rocketing. Those who have vehicles, cannot afford to fill their tanks. The country could be facing bankruptcy as early as June. And the response of the government? The politicians are now focused on the 2024 *presidential election*! This is the very definition of *insanity!* The country is in a state of crisis, and our leaders are in denial! Of course people are fed up!

A revolution requires a majority of workers, or at least a majority of advanced, class conscious workers, to recognize that revolution is necessary, and further, be prepared to die for this. The less advanced workers follow the lead of the more advanced.

It also requires the ruling class, the capitalists, to be going through a governmental crisis, so that the vast majority of workers, those who are normally apathetic, will become politically active. That is precisely the current state of affairs!

The vast majority of working people are now "watching the news", or the "Gong show in Washington", as so many refer to it. They are paying attention! Who can blame them? Their democratically elected leaders, those whom they are supposed to *respect*, are now squabbling like kids in a school playground, but without adult supervision! They are even resorting to *name calling!*

Yet these are the same people who are in control! At least, they control the tax payer money! They also make the laws! And unless they come to some sort of agreement, the *country could go broke!* It is difficult to imagine how they can come to *any* kind of agreement! This is the very definition of a *governmental crisis!*

There is no time to lose. Now it is up to conscious people, Marxists, Communists, and not just Communists, to raise the level of awareness of the most advanced strata of the proletariat. The working class must become aware of the revolutionary theories of Marx and Lenin. Now that we have the internet, and a cultured working class, this is not nearly as difficult as it used to be.

May I suggest that *all* those who consider themselves to be "on the Left", to go onto various web sites, and encourage people to download the revolutionary works of Marx and Lenin. At least, download the Communist Manifesto. The essential works of Lenin, such as State and Revolution, What Is to Be Done? Imperialism, the Highest Stage of Capitalism, and Left Wing Communism, An Infantile Disorder, can be ordered from the Internet.

May I further suggest that, once people get their hands on those revolutionary books, perhaps online discussion groups will be helpful. I expect that a great many people will find these group discussions to be enlightening.

That brings me to a significant group of people, mainly middle class, those who have a university education, are aware of the revolutionary theories of Marx and Lenin, and consider themselves to be Social Democrats, or possibly Independent Socialists. Such people tend to think that socialism is a good idea, but simply not possible.

Let me start by stating that I respect your beliefs. May I also suggest that you keep an open mind. It is very likely that your beliefs are influenced by the training you received in university. This is to say that the universities are careful to teach only the bourgeois *distortion* of the revolutionary theories of Marx and Lenin. It is only to be expected that those who have taken such university courses, should come to believe that an American Socialist Revolution could not possibly succeed.

Yet the fact of the matter is that revolutions happen, quite spontaneously, as I am sure you are well aware. The French Revolution of 1789 is perhaps most famous, although the Russian Revolution of 1905 also comes to mind. In each case, the common people just rose up, not aware of that which they were doing. I refer to this as an Act of God.

By contrast, the Russian October Revolution of 1917 was hardly spontaneous. The common people, both workers and peasants, rose up. The difference was that those people knew what they were doing! They were focused! They were class conscious! They lashed out at their class enemies! They overthrew the government of the capitalists! They then smashed the bourgeois state apparatus, and set up the Dictatorship of the Proletariat!

They were class conscious, but only because *middle class intellectuals* had brought to them the awareness of themselves *as a class,* complete with their own class interests. Those class interests include the necessity of smashing the existing state apparatus, at the time of the revolution, and replacing it with a new state apparatus, in the form of the Dictatorship of the Proletariat. In no other way can the resistance of the bourgeoisie be broken! This in turn gave rise to the first Russian Socialist Republic, the Soviet Union.

Allow me to stress the fact that it was *only* because the working class was aware of the revolutionary theories of Marx and Lenin, that the revolution was successful.

That brings me to our current situation. Assuming the American working class is equally well aware of itself *as a class,* aware of the revolutionary theories of Marx and Lenin, then the approaching revolution has every chance of success. That is hardly the current state of affairs.

That is where you come in. Feel free to ignore the bourgeois distortions of those revolutionary theories, as are taught in university. Read the true revolutionary writings of Marx and Lenin, with an open mind. You will find that they are far different from that which is taught in university!

As soon as you have a fine grasp of those theories, bring that awareness to the working class. Now that we have the internet, such a task is not terribly difficult.

The success -or failure! - of the approaching revolution is, to a large extent, in your hands! We can certainly use you now! Further, after the revolution, your services will be in great demand!

The objection may be made, that it is not fair to place this responsibility upon your shoulders. True! It is not fair! Fair has nothing to do with it! It is what it is!

That being said, allow me to state that I am confident that you will rise to the occasion. You have been living under the influence of the bourgeois ideology long enough! I refer to this as "Professor Power", and it is every bit as real as the physical force elements of repression. Now is the time to "break the invisible chains" which are binding you! Face the fact that all of the science courses, which are taught in university, especially the "Socialist" Marxist courses, are a pack of *distortions and outright lies!*

Rest assured, once you face that fact, you will likely feel a great sense of relief. At least, I did. After all, it is not just the working class that is crushed and exploited by the bourgeoisie! Also the middle class! Now is not the time to get mad! Now is the time to get even!

The best way to do that is by taking part in raising the level of awareness of the working class. Numerous Councils, otherwise known as Soviets, have taken shape, across the country. Discreetly, of course, as the government is only too anxious to destroy such working class organizations. Feel free to join such Councils.

As well, use the internet. No doubt there are countless web sites which can be used. Perhaps groups can be formed to study Marxist literature. Try not to attract the attention of the government authorities.

Bear in mind that, under far more difficult circumstances, in Russia, 1917, the common people rose up and overthrew the capitalists. The proletariat was in the minority, and not terribly cultured. The intellectual Marxists, most of whom were middle class, had to use leaflets and the spoken word, in order to raise their level of consciousness. They certainly had no Internet, as we do now! By no means everyone could read! Yet the successful socialist revolution took place, because the working class followed the revolutionary theories of Marx and Lenin.

If they could do it, then we can do it! Bear in mind that the revolution will happen, with or without the help of middle class intellectuals. Yet for the revolution to be successful, to achieve socialism, the revolutionary working class will have to follow the revolutionary theories of Marx and Lenin. There is no other way!

We will know that the working class is ready for revolution, that we are getting our message across, when the posters and banners read:

Workers of the World, Unite!

Dictatorship of the Proletariat!

Scientific Socialism

CHAPTER 7

BASILOSAURUS AND ICHTHYOSAURS: STILL WALKING THE EARTH!

It is the scientific opinion that whales once walked the earth. But then, around fifty million years ago, as these animals took to the water, they gradually lost their legs. There is some truth to this. Most species of whales have lost their legs. Most, but not all. The species known as basilosaurus still has legs, still walks on land.

It is also the scientific opinion that ichthyosaurs are extinct. The scientists refer to them as "fish lizards of the Mesozoic Era", whatever that is supposed to mean. They were also supposed to be "viviparous reptiles". This is to say that they were reptiles which "bring forth live young that have developed inside the body of the parent". (I mention this because that is the definition of "viviparous", as per the Internet.)

They indeed give birth to live young, but as they are also warm blooded animals, it stands to reason that they are mammals, not reptiles. Reptiles are cold blooded animals, while mammals are warm blooded animals, which give birth to live young.

I maintain that both basilosaurus and ichthyosaurs are still very much alive, still walking the earth. As the scientists refuse to even consider that possibility, it is up to us, common people, to do their job for them.

It is common knowledge that people who live and work around large lakes, are well aware of the fact that "something very large" is in those lakes. They are so right! In fact, there are two "somethings" in those lakes! Basilosaurus and ichthyosaurs!

Both are mammals. Both are apex predators. Both have legs. Both are nocturnal, so that they spend the daylight hours inside caves. They also spend the winter months inside caves. Both are omnivores, so that they eat flesh and vegetation. Both come out of the water after sundown and graze, during the summer months. It is very likely that they eat the same things that elephants eat. Grass, weeds, willow, leaves, brush, vegetation and everything else they can sink their teeth into. Further, both have been described as being "very long and slender".

These descriptions are accurate, as basilosaurus is estimated to be 20 metres (65 feet) long, and weigh ten to fifteen tons.

But then ichthyosaurs varied in length, from 1 to 25 meters, according to the Internet. The scientists also say that "fossils from the western United States and Canada indicate that some ichthyosaurs could exceed 13 metres (43 feet) in length." It is very likely that such is still the case!

The distinguishing feature of the ichthyosaur, is that which is referred to as a "hump" on its back. This "hump" is in reality a fin. Ichthyosaurs have fins on their backs. Basilosaurus does not have such a fin.

The fact is that a great many huge lakes, in North America, and very likely in various other parts of the world, are home to populations of these mammals. (I say "population", for lack of a better word. I have no idea what a group of ichthyosaurs are called!)

This creates a little problem, in the form of incest. Not healthy! These animals have overcome that little problem by chasing the young males away, as soon as they come of age! They are forced to "vacate the premises", to leave the lake, to travel, by river, to other huge lakes, where they can find mates! There is no other way!

This brings me to a mistake that I made several years ago. One of the boys in the village found a bone that no one here recognized. For that reason, it was taken to the University in the nearest city, that of Prince George. Someone at that University asked if "we had any whales in this territory"! My mistake was in not taking that question seriously! I thought that the idea of whales in the Central Interior, in the Rocky Mountain Trench, was ridiculous! So I ridiculed the question!

My mistake! I do not know precisely who asked that question, but whomever that was, you have my apologies. We do have whales in these mountains! It is very likely that the bone which was found, was in fact the bone of a whale, a basilosaurus.

Assuming that to be the case, then it is very likely that the whale which died was a youngster, an adolescent, who was forced out of his home lake. That is, no doubt, the most dangerous time in the life of the males. The mortality rate must be high, as they have no experience being on their own. Do or die! This whale died!

Of course, scavengers quickly tore apart the carcass, and probably one of them packed away a bone. Scavengers do that, in order to keep other scavengers from stealing it. After gnawing on it, it was abandoned. At least, that is a plausible explanation.

This brings me to the animals in Okanagan Lake, commonly referred to as Ogopogo. I use the word animals, in reference to the fact that there are almost certainly two species of animals in that lake, basilosaurus and ichthyosaur. As both are long and slender, this has given rise to a certain amount of confusion. Both species are predators, so that they are in competition with each other. For that reason, they kill each other at every opportunity. Yet as both still exist, they must be evenly matched.

Similar reports have come from other parts of the world, and in particular from Loch Ness. It is very likely that these same animals exist in that lake. One or the other, if not both.

In support of that statement, I can point out that almost one hundred years ago, one of these animals, which the local people refer to as "Nessie", was seen outside the lake. The authorities conducted an investigation, and noticed a set of tracks. These tracks were promptly *disregarded! Fools!*

Those tracks prove that this animal has legs, and explains a few things. They use those legs! A fresh water lake, by itself, cannot support a population of huge predators! There is not enough food in the lake! Granted, the fact is that they also prey upon animals which make the mistake of wandering into the lake. That still does not satisfy their "dietary requirements", so to speak. So where do they get the bulk of their nourishment?

From the meadows which border the lake! It is not just the lake which supports these animals, but the ecosystem. This is to say that the lake, along with the adjacent meadows, creeks, woodlands and swamps, comprise a huge natural body, which we refer to as an ecosystem. Further, the fact is that the health of that ecosystem is dependent on the top predators. All the more reason to preserve and protect those animals!

But as previously mentioned, the scientists refuse to even consider the possibility of the existence of these animal. Yet as they are part of our heritage, and in the interest of creating a clean environment, it is up to working people to prove that they exist. We are entitled to our wildlife! We are also entitled to a clean environment!

For that reason, we are morally obligated to prove the existence of those animal, in order to force through laws to protect them! I say "force through", because that is the last thing the capitalists want!

These animals can best be protected by cleaning up our rivers and lakes, for a start. The capitalists take great delight in polluting both, by dumping garbage and toxins from their factories, into that water. That is so much cheaper and easier than disposing of it properly!

Of course, the scientists are well aware of the existence of these animals. Yet as the loyal and devoted servants of the capitalists, they have chosen to remain silent on this point. Careers first! Do not rock the boat!

To such people, and that includes the professional people who are aware of the existence of so many animals, which are thought to be extinct, but are not, I have a word of advice. Come clean! Cut your losses!

Your days of living a lie are about to come to an end! Very soon, your lies and hypocrisy will be exposed, for all the world to see. The revolutionary motion, around the world, is gaining strength. It is just a matter of time before a Socialist Revolution takes place in a highly industrialized country, and then spreads to many other countries. At that time, your capitalist masters will not be able to protect you!

Now I also have a word of advice for a different group of people, those who are middle class intellectuals, and self-proclaimed socialists. I understand that most of you think that socialism is a good idea, but simply not possible. Your confusion is understandable.

No doubt, all of you have received a university education. As that is the case, you are *aware* of the revolutionary theories of Marx and Lenin. Bear in mind that there is a big difference between being *aware* of those theories, and having a proper scientific *understanding* of those theories.

My point is that the universities teach only the bourgeois *distortions* of the theories of Marx and Lenin. That is very likely the reason that so many middle class people, who consider themselves to be socialists, are of the opinion that socialism is a good idea, but simply not possible. They have learned this in university!

It was Marx who conducted a thorough, *scientific* examination of capitalism, and *proved* that it would, of *necessity,* give rise to socialism!

Here is the way Marx phrased it: ''And now as to myself, no credit is due to me for discovering the existence of classes in modern society, nor yet the struggle between them. Long before me, bourgeois historians had described the historical development of this class struggle, and bourgeois economists the economic anatomy of the classes. What I did that was new was to prove: 1) that the *existence of classes* is only bound up with *particular historical phases in the development of production;* 2) that the class struggle *necessarily* leads to the *Dictatorship of the Proletariat;* 3) that this Dictatorship itself only constitutes the transition to the *abolition of all classes and to a classless society".*

Take note that Marx made it clear that, under capitalism, the "class struggle *necessarily* leads to the *Dictatorship of the Proletariat"!*

The sad fact of the matter is that the university professors have a certain spiritual power, which I refer to as Professor Power. All too many people, including middle class intellectuals, are under the influence of this power. They believe that which is taught in university! It is not just the working class which is being crushed and exploited! Also the middle class!

Now it is up to the middle class to liberate themselves, to break the "invisible chains", to join the working class in their struggle for liberation!

With that in mind, may I suggest that you once again study the most important revolutionary works of Marx and Lenin, but with an open mind, while disregarding the bourgeois distortions. No doubt, you will learn, perhaps to your surprise, that the scientific socialists are correct, that in fact it is true, that capitalism *necessarily* leads to *socialism,* in the form of the *Dictatorship of the Proletariat!*

This stands in stark contrast to the university distortions of those theories. They teach the utopian socialist viewpoint that, while socialism may be a fine idea, it is simply not possible. Such is hardly the case!

Once you have a true understanding of those revolutionary theories, feel free to bring that understanding to the working class. The importance of this must be stressed. In fact, as Lenin stated, "Engels recognizes *not two* forms of the great struggle

Social Democracy is conducting (political and economic), as is the fashion among us, *but three, adding to the first two* the theoretical struggle." (italics by Lenin, while at that time Marxism was referred to as Social Democracy)

I mention this in order to stress the importance of raising the level of awareness of the proletariat.

In particular, they must be made aware of the fact that the existing state apparatus must be *smashed,* at the time of the revolution, and replaced with a new, proletarian state apparatus, in order to crush the capitalists, as they make every effort, after the revolution, to restore their "paradise lost". This state apparatus is referred to as the Dictatorship of the Proletariat. We will know we are being successful when that expression becomes common place.

Rest assured, as long as you voluntarily join the revolutionary motion, in the fight for scientific socialism, your past will not be held against you. On the contrary, your experience in the service of the capitalists can prove to be most valuable. Feel free to share that experience with the working people. This will serve to drive home the fact that classes exist, and that our differences are antagonistic. The proletariat must be persuaded that the capitalists, the billionaires, must be overthrown and crushed.

In the interests of combining theory and practice, it is perhaps best to become involved with the various Councils, or Soviets, which tend to take shape during a time of revolutionary motion. No doubt some of these Councils are involved in locating these huge animals. As I have gone into this in other articles, there is no need to repeat it here.

As well, get together with other middle class Marxist intellectuals, as well as advanced workers, and take part in the formation of a proper Communist Party, one which calls for the Dictatorship of the Proletariat. There is an urgent need for such a Party.

Rest assured that, after the successful socialist revolution, under the Dictatorship of the Proletariat, your services will be recognized and rewarded. Socialism requires professional people, managers, engineers and scientists, of all fields. For the most part, you have performed a fine job for the capitalists. Under socialism, you will do an even better job, for the proletariat. After all, the atmosphere at the workplace will be far more relaxed. You will not have to worry about office politics! We do not play such games!

Bear in mind that middle class intellectuals, including socialists, are well aware that revolutions happen, and on a regular basis. They are familiar with the Russian February Revolution of 1917, which removed the Emperor from the throne. This gave rise to the democratic republic of the Russian capitalists. That was as far as the working people could go! They could not go further, to socialism, because they were not aware of the revolutionary theories of Marx!

It was only *after* Lenin returned from exile, in April of 1917, and provided them with the proper revolutionary theory, which included the Dictatorship of the Proletariat, that the common people, the workers and poor peasants, could overthrow the capitalists, and establish a proper socialist society.

In much the same manner, the forthcoming American Revolution can also go only so far, *unless* the working class is aware that the existing state apparatus must be *destroyed*, and *replaced* with the Dictatorship of the Proletariat!

The alternative is to overthrow one set of capitalist rulers, and merely replace it with another set! Not a vast improvement!

The revolution could break out at any day. There is no time to lose.

Prepare for the Dictatorship of the Proletariat!

CHAPTER 8

FINANCIAL COLLAPSE

March 10, 2023. Black Friday. The day SVB, Silicon Valley Bank, collapsed. This day will go down in history as a day of mourning for the capitalists. The day one of the biggest banks in the country, with assets of *200 billion dollars,* collapsed, within the space of a mere *48 hours!* The beginning of the end of capitalism!

The guardians of the sacred temple of capitalism were quick to respond. The politicians and bourgeois economists, those loyal and devoted servants of the monopoly capitalists, the billionaires, the bourgeoisie, did not wait for the markets to open, the following Monday. Indeed not.

Instead, they spent a very busy weekend assuring one and all that this was an "isolated incident", despite the fact that another sizeable bank also failed, and numerous others are on the brink of bankruptcy.

The politicians were afraid that the "contagion would spread", that it would give rise to a "run on the banks", which is the very thing which happened on Saturday. They are also afraid that this could "spread to other parts of the economy", that it could lead to a "systemic failure", due to an "unstable environment".

Their fears are well grounded!

In particular, the Treasury Secretary, Janice Yellen, wasted no time in assuring people that their deposits were insured, up to 250,000, a quarter million, so that those with less than that amount of money in the bank, had nothing to fear.

True enough. All banks pay the FDIC, Federal Deposit Insurance Corporation, a fee to insure their deposits, up to that amount. All deposits above that amount are not insured. At least, not until now!

That same Treasury Secretary, as well as President Biden, swear that the taxpayers will not be "on the hook" for any bank failure. They lied!

In fact, the FDIC, in conjunction with the Federal Reserve Bank, and "back strapped" by the Treasury Department, has agreed to *insure all deposits!* The American tax payers are now responsible for all deposits, *regardless of the amount*!

To put this in perspective, the FDIC currently has 126 billion, which it can use to cover the first quarter millions of all deposits, of all banks. At least, it did. That was before it gave 110 billion to the two banks that failed. And that is just the beginning!

Numerous other banks are on the brink of collapse! Economists estimate that it may take 9 *trillion* to cover all of their deposits! That is where the tax payers come in!

Bear in mind that a trillion is one thousand billion! This is to say that the American tax payers are on the hook, thanks to Biden and Yellen, for a further *9 thousand billion!* As the national debt currently stands at 31 trillion, it could soon sky rocket to 40 trillion!

All in the interests of bailing out the banks of the billionaires, those that are Too Big to Fail! The rest of us, those who are not billionaires, are Too Small to Succeed! No one is about to bail us out!

Yet, in all fairness to the politicians, they have their "eyes on the big picture". Instead of focusing on the current fiscal crisis, which may well spread to "other parts of the economy", and lead to a "systemic failure", which could well include a default on the national debt, they are focused on the next federal election, especially the presidency. They certainly have their priorities well established! The expression "Nero fiddled while Rome burned" comes to mind!

But in the interest of winning the forth coming federal election, they have wasted no time in playing the "blame game", concerning the SVC collapse.

President Biden is blaming former President Trump for "deregulation" of banks. Economists are blaming the crisis on everything from the COVID epidemic, to inflation, high interest rates, dramatic increase in interest rates, the national debt, too much bureaucracy, too much regulation, not enough regulation, and "woke capitalism", among other things.

My personal favourite is that of "woke capitalism".

According to the Internet, "the term woke capitalism was coined to describe companies who signal support for progressive causes as a substitute for genuine changes."

True! Companies may well "signal support for progressive causes", giving it verbal recognition, commonly referred to as "lip service", while in fact, doing nothing else. To blame this verbal recognition of worthy causes, as the cause of bank failures, is utterly ridiculous!

It is *capitalism* that is the cause of banks failures! The system of *capitalism* is to blame! That is the one thing that the capitalists either *cannot*, or *will not*, face!

Despite the best efforts of the politicians, the stock prices of countless banks took a nose dive on Monday, March 13. The Internet reports that trading was halted on 30 stocks, in an effort to halt the "bloodletting". Even in Europe, economists are reporting a dramatic drop in the price of banking shares.

Some of the clearer headed bourgeois economists are warning of a possible "perfect storm of out of control inflation, recession and national debt crisis". They also expect the interest rates to rise dramatically.

Other economists, in a display of refreshing honesty, are questioning the legality of holding the tax payers responsible for the debts of all the banks. They have pointed out that it is the Congress, by which they mean the House of Representatives, which controls the money. As it is the Republicans who control the House, they may well have a thing or two, to say about the plan of Biden, a Democrat, to bail out the banks!

As is well known, the federal government is due to run out of money, very soon. They have already "hit the debt ceiling", and are now using "extraordinary measures" to keep paying the bills. That is expected to lead to a government shutdown, possibly in June, unless the debt ceiling is raised. Yet the Republican members of Congress are not at all anxious to increase the debt ceiling. They want to cut spending. They want no part of raising taxes, certainly not on the billionaires. They have no intention of paying the nine trillion that Biden has in mind, in order to save the banks!

Incidentally, it is customary for the president to exercise powers, of which he has no legal right. As long as the House and Senate allow this, he generally gets away with it. Yet this time is different. It is doubtful that the House will allow Biden to cover all bank deposits with tax payer money.

Even though Biden and Yellen, the Treasury Secretary, have agreed to cover all bank deposits, the simple fact of the matter is that the Treasury has no money! The simplest way, the easiest way, for the Congress to stop Biden and Yellen, is by doing absolutely *nothing!*

But in the interests of winning the next presidential election, it is far more likely that the Republican led House will ridicule the notion of bailing out the banks, with money they do not have!

Those two, Biden and Yellen, just made a promise they cannot possibly keep! Even if the money was available, which it is not, they do not control it!

It is perhaps significant that one economist pointed out the truth. He stated that the only way they can "bail out the banks" is by "creating money out of thin air". True! He also pointed out that this is absolutely inflationary!

I say that this is significant, because it is not in the best interests of the bourgeois economists to "blurt out the truth". Their duty is to say that which the capitalists want them to say. Any relation to the truth is strictly coincidental.

Yet as Marx and Engels pointed out, in the Communist Manifesto, "in times when the class struggle nears the decisive hour, the progress of dissolution going on within the ruling class, in fact within the whole range of old society, assumes such a violent, glaring character, that a small section of the ruling class cuts itself adrift, and joins the revolutionary class, the class that holds the future in its hands."

In our case, the "class that holds the future in its hands", is the proletariat. At least one economist has chosen to speak the truth, thus joining the "revolutionary class", the proletariat, which indicates that the "class struggle is nearing the decisive hour".

It is very likely that the clearer headed bourgeois economists are correct, in the sense that we have a "perfect storm" brewing. Yet they are wildly optimistic, as they have failed to consider the revolutionary movement! Working people are not about to put up with this!

In conclusion, we can say that the politicians are aware of the impending financial disaster, and think they have it under control. They do not.

Both political parties, Democrat and Republican, are only focused on the upcoming federal elections. Biden is determined to serve a second term, while the Republicans are equally determined to stop him.

If Biden carries through on his promise to give the banks a further 9 trillion, which he does not have, then this will lead to extreme inflation. As well, a government shutdown is ever more likely, as the Republicans are determined to block any increase to the debt ceiling. That will also very likely be followed by an American bankruptcy!

Without doubt, this would lead to a severe increase in the suffering of the common people. A Second Great Depression!

The point being that those who are predicting a "perfect storm", have no idea of just how correct they really are! This is not the nineteen thirties! Working people are not about to put up with the suffering that is part and parcel of another Great Depression!

On the contrary, working people are becoming increasingly well aware of the alternative, that of socialism. Now it is up to politically conscious people to bring to the working class the awareness of themselves as a class, with their own class interests, which involves the necessity of overthrowing the monopoly capitalists, the billionaires, the bourgeoisie, smashing the existing state apparatus, and subsequently crushing those parasites under the Dictatorship of the Proletariat. This is referred to as scientific socialism.

To put it is popular terms, the "ball is in the court of the intellectuals". Now it is up to us, those who are aware of the revolutionary theories of Marx and Lenin, to make the working class aware of the necessity of scientific socialism.

We will know that we are being successful in this when the posters and signs read:

Workers of the World, Unite!

Scientific Socialism!

Dictatorship of the Proletariat!

CHAPTER 9

CAPITALISTS RAGING AGAINST CAPITALISM!

Deception! Betrayal! Collusion! These are just a few of the charges that are being levelled against Janet Yellen, the Treasury Secretary! And not by Marxists, but by her own people! Fellow capitalists!

No Marxist has ever accused any capitalist of betrayal, because at no point has any Marxist ever trusted any capitalist! And the one and only way you can have betrayal, is by first having trust! No trust, no betrayal!

It is the small time capitalists, the middle class, the petty bourgeois, who are levelling those serious accusations against the Treasury Secretary, as well as President Biden. There is a reason for their bitterness! They have been betrayed! It is entirely possible that they have just lost everything! At least, almost everything.

Perhaps a brief summary of recent events will prove to be helpful.

On Friday, March 10 of this year, Silicon Valley Bank, SVB, collapsed. It was one of the biggest banking failures in American history. As we have previously documented, the Treasury Secretary wasted no time in assuring depositors that their deposits, in all banks, regardless of the amount, was safe. She assured one and all that, if need be, the tax payer would cover the payments, or the

Treasury would "create money out of thin air". This was made quite clear on the weekend of March 11 and 12.

Yet almost immediately, within the space of three days, the government policy, that of insuring all deposits, regardless of the amount, changed *dramatically! All* deposits of a *very few* banks would be covered, regardless of the amount! Aside from that, the deposits in the vast majority of banks, would be covered only up to 250,000!

In other words, five or six of the biggest banks in the country are to be "saved", while the rest are to be "thrown under the bus".

Yellen then went on to explain the process which would be used to determine which banks would be "saved", as opposed to those banks which would be "thrown under the bus": "If a super majority of FDIC board, and a super majority of The Fed Board, and I in consultation with the president, determine that the failure to protect uninsured depositors, would create systemic risk and significant economic and financial consequences".

In other words, it is up to Yellen and Biden to determine which banks are to succeed! Only those which are Too Big to Fail, TBTF, are to be saved. Those which are Too Small to Succeed, are to be thrown under the bus!

It is perhaps not too surprising that a great many middle class people are quite upset. After all, they have a great deal to lose! Like everything! Aside from the quarter million they may have in small banks!

The Treasury Secretary has just succeeded in drawing a clear distinction between "them", and "us". "They" are the monopoly capitalists, the billionaires, the bourgeoisie, and "we" are the "common people", the working people, the "rag tag and bob tail", the "little guy". Now that includes the middle class, the petty bourgeois, as the billionaires are determined to drive them into bankruptcy! What better way to accomplish this, than by allowing all community banks to fail?

Perhaps a little explanation is in order.

When we refer to the capitalists, we are referring to the monopoly capitalists, the billionaires and multi billionaires, technically referred to as the "bourgeoisie". We are not referring to the middle class, technically referred to as the "petty bourgeois". Granted, they are small time capitalists, but they too are being crushed and exploited by the bourgeoisie. Especially now! That is becoming clear to all of them!

Also, the word "systemic" is being frequently used, especially in regards to banks. This is to say that the capitalists are afraid that the failure of "big banks", will lead to the collapse of a great many other businesses.

By and large, the capitalists justify the "saving" of big banks, by saying that their failure, could lead to the collapse of other businesses, which they refer to as "systemic collapse".

An indication of the level of concern of the middle class people, verging on panic, is expressed on a popular Radio Show, in an unprecedented "Special Edition". They, by whom we mean the announcer and his "guest", refer to the current "insanity of the banking system". They accuse Treasury Secretary Yellen, as well as President Biden, of Deception! Betrayal! Collusion! They appear to be quite bitter! Who can blame them? Over the weekend, they were assured that all the money they had in the bank was insured. Now they realize that it was all a lie! Most of the money, which is in community banks, is not insured!

This is the reason they are screaming *Deception!* Because they have been *deceived*! They *trusted* the Treasury Secretary when she swore, on the weekend, that all their deposits were *safe!* They *believed her!* She lied, out of loyalty to the *billionaires*, so that they could draw all of *their* money out of the regional banks, before they collapsed! The middle class people have been *Betrayed!*

As for Collusion, they point out that Yellen was formerly head of The Fed, and is now head of the Treasury Department. They also give the example of a lady who was "second in command of the Federal Reserve", has now "moved to the White House as top economic advisor and director of the National Economic Council to the Biden administration". They use this as an example of *Collusion*! They think that the government is *conspiring against them!* Well of course they are! This is standard practice!

These two middle class gentlemen are among the finest, of all the bourgeois economists. They expect all regional banks to fail, including the banks with which they have deposits. In other words, they expect to soon be ruined. They say "the economy is collapsing at high speed". They also expect that a very few American banks will survive, but that will lead quickly to a "World Central Bank", complete with Digital Currency. It is nice to know what the capitalists have in mind!

Incidentally, there are those who blame this financial collapse on the COVID Epidemic. They are mistaken. As Lenin stated, in Imperialism, the Highest Stage of Capitalism, "Crises of every kind -economic crises more frequently, but not only these- in their turn increase very considerably the tendency towards monopoly and concentration".

The crisis of the COVID Epidemic did not cause this financial collapse. It merely "increased very considerably the tendency towards monopoly and concentration".

This brings us to a couple events, on that broadcast, which were rather strange. First, the announcer stated that the biggest banks were "Marxist"! As if Marxists are in charge of the biggest banks, the "pillars of capitalism"! Could that fellow be on drugs? Likely some good stuff! Perhaps he would care to share! No need to be greedy!

Then, later on in the program, he held up a book by Marx and Engels, the Communist Manifesto, no less! Whatever that boy is on, we could all use a taste!

Perhaps this can be explained by the fact that even the "most Intelligent members of the bourgeoisie" can "become muddled", so that they "cannot help creating irreparable blunders". In fact, this will "bring about the downfall of the bourgeoisie", according to Lenin, in Left Wing Communism, An Infantile Disorder.

Or it could be that they are giving thought to joining the working class, the proletariat. For that matter, they may not have much choice in the matter! From the broadcast, it is clear that they, and a great many more, just like them, are in the process of being ruined! We can certainly use such people!

As Marx and Engels stated, in the Communist Manifesto, it is such people who "supply the proletariat with fresh elements of enlightenment and progress".

The Manifesto further states that "in times when the class struggle nears the decisive hour, the process of dissolution going on within the ruling class, in fact within the whole range of old society, assumes such a violent, glaring character, that a small section of the ruling class cuts itself adrift, and joins the revolutionary class, the class that holds the future in its hands".

We are convinced that we are close to the "decisive hour"! Now is the time for those who are aware of the Revolutionary theories of Marx and Lenin, to become active! That includes those who are, or were formerly, members of the middle class! Feel free to join the proletariat, the "class that holds the future in its hands"! The middle class has no future with the bourgeoisie! The few who are not now ruined, soon will be!

The proletariat has use for such people! After the revolution, your services will be in great demand! You will be rewarded accordingly! But for the moment, focus on raising the level of awareness of the proletariat! Make them aware of the revolutionary theories of Marx and Lenin! Make them aware of themselves as a class! Make them aware of the necessity of smashing the existing state apparatus, and replacing it with the Dictatorship of the Proletariat! This can only be done through revolution! Take part in the creation of a truly Communist Party, Dictatorship of the Proletariat!

Become active! Organize demonstrations and protests! Carry signs and posters that proclaim:

Scientific Socialism!

Dictatorship of the Proletariat!

Workers of the World, Unite!

CHAPTER 10

WORLD SOCIALIST REVOLUTION UNDERWAY!

France. "The land where, more than anywhere else, the historical class struggles were each time fought out to a decision", according to Engels.

It would appear that the country of France is, once again, fighting the class struggle to a decision! This time the class struggle is between the bourgeoisie and the proletariat.

For the last three months, the government of France, led by President Macron, has been trying to enact "pension reform", as they put it, in that they want to raise the retirement age by two years, from sixty-two, to sixty-four. As the French Parliament refused to agree to this, they managed to "ram the bill through", so that it is now law.

The trade unions have responded by calling for strikes. So far this year, there have been nine strikes. Each strike has grown progressively stronger, with ever more popular support.

The strike on March 23 was exceptionally strong, with protests happening in 250 towns and cities across the country. The government estimated one million people took part in the protests, while the unions estimated the number at three and one half million.

People of all ages and all walks of life took part, so that the movement is very broad and deep. Trains were shut down and flights were delayed. The workers refused to pick up the trash, so that garbage is now piled up on the streets. Most metro lines were closed. A great many teachers joined the protests. The oil refineries were picketed. In the city of Bordeaux, the Town Hall was set on fire. As well, numerous dumpsters and vehicles have been set ablaze.

The journalists who are covering these "protests" are, for the most part, doing a rather fine job of reporting the facts. The videos support their broadcasts. On the other hand, their analysis is frequently in direct contradiction to those facts. Not too surprising, as it is in their best interest to do so.

One of these facts is that the "fury is mounting". The violent clashes are "escalating". It is "hitting the streets like a tidal wave". Hundreds of protesters have been arrested, and a great many police have been injured, some quite seriously.

One sign stated, "let us destroy what destroys us". Excellent! This is an indication that the revolutionary motion has now gone beyond opposition to "pension reform", and has also gone beyond opposition to President Macron, and the government he represents. It means there is a growing sense of class consciousness, if only in embryonic form.

It is perhaps significant that the "protesters", those who are really revolutionaries, have adopted a tactic which we have not seen before. They are using umbrellas, to good effect. While facing the riot police, they present the umbrellas as a "wall", which screens them from the police, and from between these umbrellas, are able to fire "projectiles". From the videos, it is not clear what these projectiles are, or how they are fired. Yet it is clear that these projectiles are effective, as in one video, a member of the riot police, covered in body armour, was knocked down, apparently unconscious, and dragged away by his buddies.

The press is reporting that the police are also being pelted with "molotov cocktails and acid", although there are no videos to support this. A molotov cocktail is nothing other than a glass bottle, filled with petrol, with a rag in the spout. The rag is set afire, the bottle is thrown, and as the glass breaks, the flaming petrol splashes about. Truly a revolutionary weapon!

Some of the protesters are now openly talking of revolution. As one girl stated, "No great revolution was ever achieved with a bouquet of roses". Clearly, the level of class consciousness among the working class, the proletariat, is rising!

President Macron is being referred to as a member of the "modern day royalty", a different class entirely. As the French have a history of dealing rather harshly with their royalty, this does not bode well for Macron, or the members of his class.

It is true that "France is under siege, by its own citizens", as is reported by the journalists. The country is truly "convulsing", with a "tidal wave of violence" washing over the streets. Yet the press is careful to avoid the word "revolution"!

The response of the police has been condemned by the Council of Europe, and by Amnesty International. They think the police are being too brutal.

Now the French Revolution has reached the point where some fire fighters have joined the revolutionaries. The experience of previous revolutions suggests that before long, the police will also join the revolution.

Now unions are calling for another general strike, on March 28. Clearly, a revolution is happening, yet it is not the duty of trade unions to lead a revolution.

This is not to denigrate the role of trade unions. By no means. To put it in popular terms, "the right tool for the job!"

As Lenin explained, quite clearly, in Left Wing Communism, An Infantile Disorder, "The trade unions were a tremendous step forward for the working class in the early days of capitalist development, inasmuch as they marked a transition from the workers' disunity and helplessness to the *rudiments* of class organization". He went on to say that it is the role of trade unions to "educate and school people, to give them *all round development and an all-round* training, so that they *are able to do everything*" (italics by Lenin)

He went on to point out, "the development of the proletariat did not, and could not, proceed anywhere in the world otherwise than through the trade unions, through reciprocal action between them and the Party of the working class".

Of course, the "Party of the working class" is the Communist Party. Further, the only *true* Communist Party is one which calls for the Dictatorship of the Proletariat, the "touchstone" of a true Marxist. It is up to the Communist Party to help the proletariat develop through "reciprocal action", with the trade unions.

This brings us to the role of the Communist Party. Lenin refers to this as the *"Revolutionary Party of the Proletariat,* the *highest* form of proletarian class organization". It is up to the Communist Party to "educate and guide the trade unions", as they are an "indispensable 'school of Communism' and a preparatory school that trains proletarians to exercise their dictatorship, an indispensable organization of the workers" (italics by Lenin).

Perhaps as a means of stressing the difficulty of this task, Lenin went on to say that it is the "necessity, the absolute necessity, for the Communist Party, the vanguard of the proletariat, its class conscious section, to resort to changes of tact, to conciliation and compromises with the various groups of proletarians, with the various parties of the workers and small masters. It is entirely a matter of *knowing how* to apply these tactics in order to *raise* -not lower- the *general* level of proletarian class consciousness, revolutionary spirit, and ability to fight and win." (italics by Lenin)

We hope that clarifies the roles of trade unions, as well as that of the Communist Party.

It would appear that there are a number of strong trade unions in France, but no true French Communist Party. Of course, by this we mean one that calls for the Dictatorship of the Proletariat.

This is a serious matter, as the *one and only* way the revolution can succeed, is through the Dictatorship of the Proletariat! True, the existing government, referred to as the Macron Regime, must be overthrown. Yet that is not enough! This government merely represents the monopoly capitalists, the billionaires, the bourgeoisie. The existing state apparatus, which has been set up, by the capitalists, in order to crush and exploit the working people, must be *smashed!* It must be then replaced by another state apparatus, in order to crush the "desperate and determined" resistance of the bourgeoisie, as they try, after the revolution, to restore their "paradise lost". This new state apparatus is known as the Dictatorship of the Proletariat. The worst night mare of every capitalist!

It is entirely possible likely! - that there are a number of social chauvinists in France, working diligently, in order to divert the revolutionary motion onto some harmless course of "social reform". By "harmless", we mean harmless to the bourgeoisie! Social chauvinists are socialists in words only, chauvinists in deeds! They are among the most loyal, devoted servants of the bourgeoisie!

Lenin refers to these people as "Economists", or "Mensheviks", and documents the struggle he had with them, in his excellent article, What Is to Be Done?

But then capitalism gives rise to such people, in all countries! It is up to true scientific socialists, Marxists, Communists, to expose these people. They must be rooted out, as they are counter revolutionary.

Now it is up to class conscious people, those who are aware of the revolutionary theories of Marx and Lenin, to bring to the working class, the proletariat, the awareness of themselves as a class, with their own class interests. By and large, this means middle class people, as those revolutionary theories are taught only in University.

Yet now that we have been blessed with the internet, the situation has changed, quite dramatically. Many of those revolutionary works can be directly downloaded, such as the Communist Manifesto. Others can be ordered online. As well, with the use of email, documents can be sent, quite easily. It is no longer necessary to resort to the written word, on paper, referred to as leaflets. This makes the job of Communists ever so much easier!

Further, as mentioned in other articles, due to the "process of dissolution" going on within the capitalist class, a great many middle class people are joining the working class. Some voluntarily, others not so voluntarily. It matters not, as long as they bring with them their awareness of the revolutionary theories of Marx and Lenin.

To such people, we can only suggest that it is a "win - win" situation. You have nothing to lose! After the revolution, your experience and training will be in demand! You will be rewarded accordingly! Your past, in the service of the capitalists, will not be held against you!

That brings us to one more detail, which is conspicuous by its absence. That is Soviets, or Councils. We do not know the name in French. Yet revolution, or more accurately, revolutionary motion, gives rise to such organizations. They have almost certainly made an appearance, yet there is no mention of them, on the Internet. We can only suggest that Communists become active within these strictly proletarian creations.

It is clear that the French working people are now in the vanguard of the World Socialist Revolutionary motion. We can only hope that they will honour their revolutionary ancestors, the Communards, the heroic workers of Paris, those who took part in the Paris Commune, of 1871! The example of the Paris Communards will forever serve as an inspiration to all revolutionaries!

CHAPTER 11

TRUMP BEING CHARGED!

On March 30, 2023, American history was made. For the first time, a former president was charged with a crime. Donald Trump, in fact, was charged with over thirty crimes, which have yet to be disclosed.

The press is quite cheerfully reporting on all the gruesome details. That is awfully sweet of them, but the fact remains that most common people are not Philadelphia lawyers. For that reason, if no other, many people are quite confused. As that is the case, and as so many people are interested, it is time to explain a few things.

We can start by facing the fact that the journalists are now crowing about Trump being ''indicted'' by a Manhattan Grand Jury. This is a legal term which just means that he has been charged. Perish forbid they should just use plain and simple English!

There is a big difference between a Grand Jury and a regular jury.

A Grand Jury is composed of twenty-three citizens, supposedly chosen at random. We are concerned with the Grand Jury which issued ''indictments'' for Trump, in New York City.

The Manhattan District Attorney, Alvin Bragg, is the prosecutor. He ''convened'' a Grand Jury. He then presented evidence, to that Grand Jury, in support of his contention that one or more crimes has been committed, by Donald Trump. This evidence included witnesses. We have no way of knowing what was said, as the only people who are allowed into the room are the prosecutor, the jurors, witnesses and a court reporter.

It is significant that no judge or defense lawyers are allowed into the room, so that there cannot possibly be any cross examination of any witness. Further, the defense cannot present any evidence. In fact, the people who are the focus of the investigation may not even be aware that they are being investigated!

After Bragg, the DA, presented his case, he asked the Grand Jury for an indictment, or a number of indictments, in order to charge Trump. Apparently they responded, with a certain amount of enthusiasm.

In all cases, the Grand Jury is told that if they consider it "more likely than not", that the defendant is guilty, then they should vote to indict. A simple majority is required for an indictment. This means that if only twelve jurors, out of twenty-three, vote to indict, then the defendant is charged.

It should come as no great surprise to anyone, to find that the Grand Jury almost always votes to indict. That is the source of the ridiculous expression that "a Grand Jury can vote to indict a ham sandwich".

Perhaps the strangest part of these proceedings, is the fact that the alleged "crime" in question, that of paying "hush money" to a porn star, is nothing more than a misdemeanor, one which took place seven years ago. By law, the maximum penalty for a misdemeanor is one year in jail, but this almost never happens. Yet the DA is arguing that the payment was documented incorrectly, and was used to commit another crime, a felony. As that is the case, the "hush money payment" was also a felony.

A great many legal experts are suggesting that the DA is "standing on rather shaky legal ground". This is their polite way of saying that they expect the courts to throw out the charges. That is certainly the goal of the lawyers who work for Trump!

By law, a felony is a serious crime, usually punishable by imprisonment for a term of several years. By contrast, a misdemeanor is a less serious crime, so that those who are convicted, rarely go to jail. No wonder the lawyers who represent Trump are trying to get those felony charges thrown out of court!

As yet, we do not know just which charges Trump is facing, as the indictments are "under seal", to use the legal expression.

The next step in this "gong show" involves the "accused", in this case Trump. He is expected to "surrender" to the police. This is to say that he is expected to "present himself" to the police, at a certain agreed upon time.

His lawyers are trying to work out the details, which are complicated by the fact that he is under the protection of the Secret Service! Just how the Secret Service is supposed to protect Trump, while in police custody, or even *in jail,* is a mystery!

After Trump "surrenders himself", to the police, he can expect to be "booked". This is to say that he will be treated in the same manner as all other "criminal suspects". He will be photographed and fingerprinted!

Then he will be taken to the Supreme Court of the state of New York, in the borough of Manhattan, for his "arraignment". In other words, he will be taken into court, escorted by the police, and brought before the judge. It remains to be seen if he will be wearing handcuffs!

While in court, before a judge, the criminal charges against Trump will be read aloud. At that point, he will become aware of the charges against him. And so will we!

He will then be expected to "enter a plea". No doubt that will be a plea of "not guilty". This is all part of the arraignment process.

At that time, there is also something referred to as "discovery", so that a prosecutor must turn over all evidence to the defense attorneys.

We can expect Trump to be released on "PR Bond", also known as "personal recognizance bond", which is a type of bail bond that does not require the defendant to pay any money up front. Instead, the court issues an order releasing the defendant from custody on the condition that they agree to appear for all scheduled court appearances.

It is only those who cannot afford to post the bail bond, who are required to come up with that money! Those who are filthy rich, are relieved of that burden!

The journalists are speculating that the lawyers for Trump will "file a motion" to have all charges dropped, or more likely, a great many motions. After all, there are "higher courts". This particular court is the Supreme Court of the state of New York, not of the country. As Trump can afford to hire a small army of lawyers, he can no doubt drag this through the courts for many years, if need be.

Strangely enough, these charges, in the state of New York, are considered to be the "weakest". Several other investigations have also been going on, for several years, but as yet, no prosecutor has "worked up the courage" to charge Trump. Now that Bragg has dared to perform his duty, this may well "open the flood gates".

Possibly the most serious charges may soon be placed by the state of Georgia, in that they are considering charging Trump with "attempting to overturn the federal election of 2020". Such an accusation borders on treason!

It is reported that a Grand Jury, in that state, has completed their investigation, on January 24 of this year. Now it is up to the District Attorney to "take the plunge", to press charges against Trump. Feel free to "grow a set"!

Legal experts said that Trump may have violated at least three state election laws, all of which are very serious. A conviction of any one of those charges could result in a lengthy prison sentence.

On the federal level, the United States District Attorney may charge that Trump "improperly retained classified records" at his Florida estate, after he left office, and then "attempted to obstruct a federal investigation".

The House of Representatives has requested that the Justice Department also charge Trump for the role he played, in that which they refer to as the "January 6 Insurrection". For that reason, the Justice Department is also "investigating his actions in the 2020 election".

As well, the Attorney General of the state of New York is reportedly investigating Trump, and his family, for allegations of various acts of fraud, in their business dealings. They claim that Trump and his company, Trump Organization, owe them 250 million.

They also maintain that they have uncovered evidence of "criminal wrong doing", which was promptly referred to the federal prosecutors and the IRS. Another one who should "grow a set"!

Those people certainly know how to "pass the buck"!

It is entirely possible that the investigation, by the state of New York, into allegations of fraud, by Trump and his family, may become his biggest headache. Trump may not be the only one who could be facing a lengthy stay in prison!

While there is a law forbidding married couples from testifying against each other, there is no law against children testifying against their parents! Further, there is a vicious rumor to the effect that at least one of his children has been spending some "quality time" with the FBI! It is doubtful that these were social calls!

Numerous -former! – "business associates" of Trump can testify to the fact that he does not hesitate to throw anyone "under the bus", if it suits his purpose. It is entirely possible that he has taught his children well! Trump may soon find himself joining so many others, "under the bus"! Thrown there by one of his own children! One who is a "chip off the old block"! The old "better you than me"!

We have decided to go into considerable detail, concerning the charges against Trump, only because the common people are interested in this. Not for a moment, do we believe that sending Trump to jail, will change anything!

As is well known, those who are extremely rich, the billionaires, are above the law. They can do almost anything they like, and get away with it. So what is going on with Trump?

Even though Trump is a billionaire, a member of a class which we refer to as the bourgeoisie, the class of people who are in charge, he is considered to be a renegade.

As he is a "loose cannon", the other members of his class have decided that he must go. For that reason, they have given the "go ahead" to various District Attorneys, across the country. Send Trump to jail! It is now "open season" on Donald Trump!

In fact, this is just part of the "process of dissolution going on within the ruling class", as the capitalists are losing their "grip" on power.

It is becoming abundantly clear that capitalism is in a state of crisis. Further, the capitalists can no longer rule in the old way. It is also just as clear that the "lower classes", the working people, are no longer content to live in the old way, and are demanding change. This is the very definition of a revolutionary situation!

Now for the revolution to be successful, it is necessary that a "majority of the class conscious, thinking and politically active workers, should fully realize that revolution is necessary", according to Lenin.

To such people, the working people who are demanding change, we can only stress the importance of becoming class conscious. Feel free to read the most important works of Marx and Lenin, including the Communist Manifesto, the Essential Works of Lenin, and Left Wing Communism, An Infantile Disorder.

Those works stress the importance of revolution, of overthrowing the monopoly capitalists, of smashing the existing state apparatus and setting up a new state apparatus, in the form of the Dictatorship of the Proletariat. That is necessary, in order to keep them from returning to power.

Bear in mind that the only reason this article was focused on Trump, is because that is what people are talking about. Capitalism is capitalism, regardless of the individual who is president. All presidents serve the same class.

The revolution will break out soon. That much is clear. What is not clear, is whether or not it will be successful. That largely depends upon the most advanced strata of the proletariat.

With that in mind, may we suggest such slogans as:

Workers of the World, Unite!

Dictatorship of the Proletariat!

Scientific Socialism!

CHAPTER 12

CONCERNING WARS WHICH ARE NECESSARY AND JUST

As is well known, there is a certain news outlet which is considered to be supremely "Right Wing". No one has ever accused them of being "Leftist", of being sympathetic towards socialism. They are one of the most outspoken defenders of capitalism, and appear to be quite proud of that fact.

Yet it is also a fact that they tend to give a very accurate description of that which is taking place. They even dare to report on events, which the other main stream news outlets tend to ignore.

One example of such an event, which the other news outlets ignored, was the recent appearance of the Speaker of the House, Nancy Pelosi, in New York City. It is very likely that the other news outlets did not cover the event, for fear of offending certain members of the capitalist class.

There followed an exchange, between Nancy Pelosi, and various members of the audience, which I consider to be of the utmost importance. It reveals the level of passion of the working class, which is an indication of the strength of the Revolutionary motion.

Also of importance, is the reporting and analysis of the journalists. The reporting is excellent; the analysis is faulty.

For that reason, I have attempted to repeat it, as accurately as possible.

Journalist: "Every once in a while, there is a moment in history when both sides of the political aisle wake up. We have reached a turning point."

The journalists are right when they say that "we have reached a turning point". That "turning point" is the revolution! The common people, the working class, the proletariat, is "waking up"! That is indeed "one side of the political aisle", commonly referred to as the "Left"!

This is not to say that we have reached a "moment in history" when "both sides of the political aisle wake up"! The "other side of the political aisle", the monopoly capitalists, the billionaires, the bourgeoisie, the "Right", are by no means "waking up"! On the contrary, they remain as reactionary as ever!

The journalists went on to give the example of Trump, who once referred to the Iraq war as a "mistake". Their conclusion?

Journalist: "That was a moment the levee broke, when the liberals and conservatives realized there is no Right and Left! It is more establishment and everyone else. The power players in the White House did not change. Nancy Pelosi is still Nancy Pelosi. The Left is not having it now."

On the contrary, at the "moment the levee broke", the difference between the Right and the Left, the proletariat and the bourgeois, became quite sharp and clear!

The "establishment", as the journalists refer to the "power players in the White House", also include the politicians in Washington, and not just the White House! Indeed, they "did not change"! They have merely "revealed their true colours"! They stand more exposed! They are, most emphatically, the Right! The differences now are sharp and clear! The Right represents the capitalists, the billionaires, the bourgeoisie!

Those whom the journalists refer to as "everyone else", are the common people, the members of the public, the working people, the "liberals and conservatives", as well as the middle class, the petty bourgeois, the Left!

To deny the existence of the "Right" and the "Left", is to deny the existence of classes!

Remarkably enough, the same journalists who are such staunch supporters of capitalism, have just now classified themselves as members of the Left! As yet, they are not aware of this.

They further went on to report that at the meeting, the spectators "heckled" Nancy Pelosi mercilessly. They called her a "War Criminal"! She was accused of "trying to start a war with China", by "going to Taiwan"! She was told that "she belongs in the depths of hell"! She was also accused of "getting us into a war with Iraq and Afghanistan". She was called "War Hungry Nancy"! Other accusations were also made, but were supremely vulgar, and do not bear to be repeated. Last but not least, she was accused of supporting the war in Ukraine!

Such accusations, in a public setting, are nothing short of shocking! It is doubtful that Nancy Pelosi has ever been treated before, in such a manner! As the former Speaker of the House, second in line to the presidency, she is accustomed to being treated with a great deal of respect! Yet the audience voiced their complete contempt for her!

Such a public outburst can take place only as a result of the revolutionary movement!

Strangely enough, the journalists have even gone so far as to lump two members of "The Squad", AOC and Hakim Jeffries, with Nancy Pelosi, as "War Mongers", as they "support the war in Ukraine".

In all fairness to these particular journalists, I can only stress, that they accurately report the facts. From these facts, they then attempt to draw certain conclusions. At that point, they become completely confused.

One of their more ridiculous conclusions is that the "progressives are now pro war", no longer part of the "anti-war movement".

They have come to this conclusion, as a result of the "progressives" calling for support for the Ukrainian people, in their fight against the Russian invasion.

This shows that these journalists, all of whom are petty bourgeois, cannot think in class terms! For that reason, they have managed to work themselves into a "muddle", to use the expression of Lenin. They think that all of those on the Left are "anti-war". Pacifists! Such is hardly the case!

True, the "progressives", by whom they mean those on the "Left", were opposed to the American wars of aggression in Iraq and Afghanistan. This is not to say that those on the Left are pacifists! It just means that the Left is opposed to wars of aggression, because they are "unjust wars".

The war in Ukraine is also an "unjust war", in the sense that Russia is trying to conquer the country. The Left is also opposed to this war of aggression, this unjust war. For that reason, it is correct to support the people of Ukraine, in their defense of their country.

Yet the journalists think that because the Left opposed the American wars of aggression, we are "anti-war". They cannot understand the reason we are calling on all people to support the Ukrainians, in their war to defend their country, against the Russian aggression.

The reason is that the Russians had no right to invade Ukraine. It is a war of conquest. This makes it an unjust war, on the part of the Russians. The Ukrainians have every right to defend their country.

Perhaps they are confused by the fact that the Right is also supporting the people of Ukraine, in their attempt to defend their country. In fact, the American government is sending vast amounts of weapons and ammunition, to the country of Ukraine! For their own reasons, mind you!

Perhaps a comparison to a similar situation, may prove to be helpful.

The current situation is similar to that of Russia, in early 1917, a time of revolution. Also a time of mass confusion!

As is well known, at that time, the "great slaughter" of working people was taking place. It has gone down in history as the First World War. The monopoly capitalists, the imperialists, of the most highly developed countries of the world, the so called "Great Powers", were fighting among themselves, in an effort to redivide the world.

One completely unexpected result of this, which is referred to as "collateral damage", was the collapse of the Romanov dynasty! Those whom had ruled the huge Russian empire, for three centuries, were deposed, within the space of a mere eight days! Incredible!

This requires a little explanation.

As Lenin stated, in the first of his "Letters from Afar", in reference to the collapse of the Romanov dynasty, that "every abrupt turn in history, and this applies to every revolution, presents such a wealth of content, unfolds such unexpected and specific combinations of forms of struggle and alignment of forces of the contestants, that to the lay mind there is much that must appear miraculous."

He went on to explain that there were a "number of factors of world historic importance" which led to the "collapse of the tsarist monarchy, in a few days".

Among other things, this required a "great, mighty and all powerful 'stage manager', capable, on the one hand, of vastly accelerating the course of world history, and on the other, of engendering worldwide crises of unparalleled intensity - economic, political, national and international…This all powerful 'stage manager', this mighty accelerator, was the imperialist world war".

May I suggest that the modern day equivalent of the "imperialist world war", the "all powerful stage manager", the "mighty accelerator", that which is "capable of vastly accelerating the course of world history", is a combination of the COVID-19 Virus, and the financial crisis, which is currently sweeping the world.

As well, a great many people have taken part in the Occupy Movement of recent memory. They are now seasoned veterans! They have no illusions! They know what to expect! We may think of them as the equivalent of the veterans of the Russian Revolution of 1905. Those veterans were another factor in the rapid overthrow of the Romanovs!

On that subject, in early 1917 Russia, there was, as Lenin stated, "a profound proletarian and mass popular movement of a Revolutionary character …for *bread,* for *peace,* for *real freedom*". (italics by Lenin) For that reason, the common people, the workers and peasants, wanted Tsar Nicholas gone!

At the same time, the Russian capitalists also wanted Tsar Nicholas gone, but for completely different reasons! The capitalists wanted *war!*

They were afraid that Tsar Nicholas would sign a "separate" peace treaty with Germany! So the Russian capitalists, working with the British and French capitalists, through their embassies in the capitol of Saint Petersburg, organized a plot to depose Tsar Nicholas.

Lenin referred to this in the following terms: "as a result of an extremely unique historical situation, *absolutely dissimilar currents, absolutely heterogeneous* class interests, *absolutely contrary* political and social strivings have *merged*". (italics by Lenin)

The lesson here, is that there are times when the goals of the Left "merge" with the goals of the Right. This is not to say that we are allies. We are not. We are bitter enemies. It is to say that our goals have "merged".

This brings us to our current situation, which involves the war in Ukraine.

Those of us who are on the Left, consider this to be an "unjust war", as Russia has invaded the country, in an attempt to conquer it. For that reason, those who are on the Left are calling for all people to support the people of Ukraine, in their war of defense, against the Russian invaders. That is a fact.

It is also a fact that those who are on the Right, by whom I mean the American government, are also supporting the Ukrainian people, in their war against the Russian invaders! They are shipping vast quantities of military hardware to Ukraine! For their own reasons! The American imperialists do not want the Russian imperialists to seize control of Ukraine! They want to have Ukraine join NATO, so that they can instead control Ukraine!

This is another example of "absolutely contrary political strivings" merging! The Left wants to assist Ukraine in their struggle against Russian invaders, so that they can remain independent, while the Right wants to assist Ukraine, so that they can subdue the country!

Without doubt, there are also a great many Leftist people, in Russia, who are also against the war in Ukraine. In this way, they too are supporting the people of Ukraine.

This brings us to the subject of war. In particular, not all wars are the same. Wars of conquest are considered to be "unjust wars", and it is correct for people on the Left to oppose those wars.

Just as the Russian invasion of Ukraine is an example of an unjust war, so too the American invasions of Iraq and Afghanistan were examples of unjust wars. The opposition, by the Left, was correct, in those cases.

Such wars of conquest, "unjust wars", stand in sharp contrast to wars which are "just". These wars include that of national liberation, as well Revolutionary Wars!

We must stress that a true socialist, a Marxist, a Communist, is not a pacifist, an opponent of all war. Each war must be assessed, based on the facts, on the *class character* of that war. In each case, we must consider the events which led up to that particular war, the classes that are waging the war, and to what purpose.

In the case of the current war, which is raging in Ukraine, it is clear that the Russian imperialists, led by Putin, invaded the country of Ukraine, for the purpose of conquering the country. For that reason, we refer to this as an "unjust war", on the part of Russia.

The citizens of Ukraine are fighting this unjust war, as they do not want to be conquered. They have no choice in the matter. They are not about to bow down to the Russian invaders!

Now the American Left is *supporting* the Ukrainian people, in their defensive war, against the Russian imperialists. This too is correct.

No doubt, at the same time, within Russia, there is a strong anti-war movement, against the Russian war of aggression. This is similar to the American anti-war movement, during the time of the wars with Iraq and Afghanistan.

Now if only the petty bourgeois journalists could understand that!

This confusion, among the journalists, is not at all surprising, but it is unfortunate.

I say not surprising, because they are middle class, petty bourgeois, and the members of that class frequently get confused. Yet it is unfortunate, as they tend to spread their confusion.

To this day, a great many common people still support Trump. This particular news outlet is a strong supporter of Trump. For that reason, a great many working people watch this news outlet, and are bound to become confused by that which the journalists state. After all, it makes no sense.

In conclusion, we can only stress the fact that classes exist. The working class, the proletariat, family farmers, and at least the lower strata of the middle class, the petty bourgeois - although ever more middle class people are moving to the Left! - are people whom I refer to as "common people", the members of the "Left".

By contrast, the billionaires, the monopoly capitalists, the bourgeoisie, also known as imperialists, along with their supporters, are members of the "Right".

As well, there are different types of war. Wars of aggression are "unjust wars", and must be opposed. By contrast, there are "just wars". These include wars of national liberation, and definitely Revolutionary Wars.

These Revolutionary Wars we must embrace.

Especially as we are currently on the brink of a World Revolutionary Socialist War!

CHAPTER 13

CONCERNING THE IMPORTANCE OF PROLETARIAN ORGANIZATIONS

In my previous article, I argued that the current situation, around the world, is comparable to that which existed in Russia, in early 1917. Immediately after the overthrow of Tsar Nicholas, the political climate can best be described in one word: Revolutionary!

At that time, the revolution was raging in Russia. The "First Revolution", which was a reference to the overthrow of Tsar Nicholas, was widely anticipated to be followed by a "Second Revolution", one which was expected to overthrow the capitalists.

Of course, Lenin was following events, as best he could, from "afar", as he was still in exile. Yet even with the scarce news reports at his disposal, he was able to get a pretty good grasp of the events, as they unfolded in Russia.

He noted that the "slogan of the moment" was "organization". Yet as that slogan contained no class content, it meant nothing. After all, organization is always needed.

For that reason, most working people are already organized in trade unions, as well as clubs of various sorts, such as sports, books, dancing, cycling and so forth. This is a natural result of working people wanting to associate with others, those who share the same interests. There is nothing wrong with this.

The trouble comes when leaders insist that workers *confine themselves* to such organizations. That is the very thing the capitalists want, in order to strengthen their rule. They are determined that the "workers *should not go beyond their ordinary 'legal' organizations*", according to Lenin. (italics by Lenin)

Fortunately, in 1917, the Russian common people, by whom I mean the workers and peasants, were not listening to such leaders, those who were trying to limit them to their "legal" organizations. Indeed, not!

Instead, they took a "page from the book" of the previous Russian Revolution, that of 1905. They set up a *Soviet of Workers Deputies!* What is more, they expanded upon the Soviets, which had first been created in 1905. Indeed, they created a Soviet of Soldiers Deputies, a Soviet of Poor Peasants Deputies, as well as a Soviet of Rural Wage Workers Deputies.

For the benefit of those who are not aware, the word Soviet means Council, in English. These Soviets, or Councils, are created as a result of Revolutionary Motion.

As various revolutions, or perhaps more accurately, revolutionary motion, is raging in various countries around the world, it is reasonable to assume that these Soviets have also spontaneously appeared.

For his part, Lenin stressed the importance of these Soviets. As he phrased it, "The prime and most important task, and one that brooks no delay, is to set up organizations of this kind in all parts of Russia, without exception, for all trades and strata of the proletarian and semi proletarian population, without exception".

That is as true now, as when it was first written. Soviets of Workers, Peasants, Military Personnel and Rural Workers must be established, in the various countries of the world, which are experiencing Revolutionary Motion.

I use the expression "Military Personnel", instead of "Soldiers", as it is possible that various branches of the military may object to being referred to as "Soldiers". Some of them may prefer to be referred to as Sailors, Marines, Coast Guard, Airmen or even Military. That is entirely up to them.

For that matter, here in North America, we have family farmers who may object to the name "peasant". So perhaps the term Soviets of Family Farmers is acceptable. Of course, the industrial farmers should not be allowed to join those Soviets, as they correspond to the "kulaks", rich peasants, the Russian rural bourgeoisie.

That "begs the question": What is the function of the Soviets? The answer, according to Lenin, is that they "must be regarded as organs of insurrection, of Revolutionary Rule". This calls for a little explanation.

A couple of years earlier, in October of 1915, in his article "Several Theses", Lenin went into this in some detail. As it is so important, we have decided to quote the pertinent parts here, while not going into the parts which dealt with the Russian autocracy:

"We consider that the consolidation and extension of Social Democratic work among the proletariat and its extension to the rural proletariat, the rural poor and the army are the immediate and pressing tasks. It is Revolutionary Social Democracy's most pressing task to develop the incipient strike movement...

"Soviets of Workers Deputies and similar institutions must be regarded as organs of insurrection, of revolutionary rule. It is only in connection with the development of a mass political strike and with an insurrection, and in the measure of the latter's preparedness, development and success, that such institutions can be of lasting value.

"Only a revolutionary democratic Dictatorship of the Proletariat and the peasantry can form the social content of the impending Revolution in Russia...We have urged and still urge the absolute need, in any and all circumstances, for a *separate* organization for rural *proletarians*...

"We consider it admissible for Social Democrats to join a provisional Revolutionary government with the democratic petty bourgeoisie, but *not* with the revolutionary chauvinists...

"Revolutionary chauvinism is based on the class position of the petty bourgeoisie. The latter always vacillates between the bourgeoisie and the proletariat....

"Our slogan is: Against the chauvinists, even if they are revolutionary and republican - *against* them, and *for* an alliance of the international proletariat for the Socialist Revolution...

"The international solidarity of the revolutionary proletariat is a *fact,* despite the scum of opportunism and social chauvinism." (all italics by Lenin)

Incidentally, at the time Lenin was writing this, all Marxists were referred to as Social Democrats, as they were fighting for Democracy as well as Socialism. Later they became known as Bolsheviks, and then Communists.

By the social chauvinists, he is referring to those who are socialists in words, chauvinists in deeds. Their goal is to take over the existing state apparatus, at the time of the revolution, and set themselves up, as the new rulers.

Note that Lenin referred to Soviets as "organs of Insurrection, of Revolutionary rule". They must be as broad as possible, embracing all common people. That includes urban, city workers, those in industry, as well as those in rural, country areas, such as farm laborers. It is also important to set up Soviets in the military, as most enlisted personnel are working people. As well, there should be a Soviet of Poor Peasants, or Family Farmers. In fact, all working people, in all walks of life, must be organized in Soviets.

There is a good reason for this. At the time of the revolution, the existing state apparatus, that which has been set up, by the capitalists, for the purpose of crushing the working people, must be *smashed!* This is to say that the "organs of government", by which we mean the police force, army and bureaucracy, must be *abolished!*

It may come as a great surprise, to so many people, to find that Lenin referred to this state apparatus as a "magnificent organization"! But only because that is precisely the case! After all, it is the creation of the entire bourgeoisie, and the entire bourgeois intellectuals, in all capitalist countries! Further, they have had several hundred years to perfect this state apparatus!

In fact, this bourgeois state "machine" -as that is the word the capitalists use- is so precious, it is closely guarded! Cherished and protected! The capitalists consider this state "machine" to be their "Crown Jewel"! The Crown Jewels of the royalty could not be more closely guarded!

As Lenin pointed out, "All bourgeois revolutions merely perfected *this* state machine, merely transferred *it* from the hands of one party to those of another." (italics by Lenin)

To think that this "state machine", this closely guarded "Crown Jewel" of the capitalists, is the very thing that we must destroy, at the time of the revolution! That is indeed a "tall order"!

Yet we are not anarchists, those who are opposed to any sort of state apparatus. On the contrary, we are well aware that a different sort of state apparatus is required. After all, the capitalists can be counted upon, after the revolution, to make every effort to "restore their paradise lost". They are so predicable! They will stoop to any depth, to any deception, in their efforts to return to power!

The capitalists are not to be under estimated! After all, they managed to return to power, in the Soviet Union, after the death of Stalin. Not only that, but they also managed to return to power, in China, after the death of Mao!

As I have covered that in a separate article, and have suggested a course of action to prevent such a further reversal, there is no need to repeat it here.

For the purposes of this article, it must be stressed that at the time of the revolution, after the capitalists are overthrown, after the bourgeois state apparatus has been smashed, a new state apparatus must be set up. "But not the *kind of state* the bourgeoisie has created everywhere", as Lenin stated. (italics by Lenin)

Instead, we need a state apparatus of a different sort, one that will *crush* the capitalists. We must substitute a new one, "by *merging* the police force, the army and the bureaucracy with *the entire armed people!*" as per Lenin (italics by Lenin)

Lenin goes on to say that "the proletariat must organize and arm *all* the poor, exploited sections of the population in order that they *themselves* should take the organs of state power directly into their own hands, in order that *they themselves should constitute* these organs of state power." (italics by Lenin)

As Lenin pointed out, after the revolution, we will need "a militia that will really embrace the entire people, be really universal, and be led by the proletariat!" He referred to this as the "task of the day".

He went on to say that what we need is a "genuine *people's* militia, one that first, consists of the *entire* population, of all citizens of *both* sexes; and second, one that combines the functions of a people's army with police functions" (italics by Lenin)

This new, soon to be created state apparatus, has been given the title of the Dictatorship of the Proletariat. After the completion of the Socialist Revolution, and the smashing of the bourgeois state apparatus, this proletarian state apparatus will be set up, as a means of crushing the capitalists, of exercising dictatorship over them.

In my opinion, the most important thing now, is to prepare for the Dictatorship of the Proletariat.

With that in mind, Soviets must be set up in all areas of the country. By that I mean, all countries that are in the midst of revolutionary motion. Further, those Soviets must be trained, armed and equipped. The most advanced workers must be placed in positions of leadership. Such advanced workers, those with little or even no training, will be placed in positions of authority, after the revolution. Any training they receive now, will prove to be most valuable.

As I have gone into this in previous articles, there is no need to repeat it here.

In conclusion, we can only state the fact that most, if not all, of the most highly industrialized countries of the world, are in the midst of a crisis. All are deeply in debt. The banks are also "overextended", to use the polite term. Both the banks and countries, are on the verge of bankruptcy. Even the finest bourgeois economists are admitting the "possibility" of world financial collapse. In fact, it is a certainty.

It is also a fact that the working class, around the world, is in revolutionary motion. Excellent! Yet that is not enough.

In previous writings, I have compared the class struggle -or war, more accurately! - to two boxers, slugging it out. Yet one boxer is blindfolded. This gives the other boxer a huge advantage.

Of course, in this extremely over simplified manner, I have compared the working class, which is not aware of itself as a class, with its own class interests, to the capitalist class, which is supremely well aware of itself, as a class. Further, the capitalists are well aware of the revolutionary theories of Marx and Lenin. That includes the theory of the Dictatorship of the Proletariat. They have learned this in university.

By contrast, the working class is largely barred from university, and the revolutionary theories of Marx and Lenin, are not taught in public schools. So of course the working class is not aware, and cannot be aware, of those revolutionary theories. It follows that the workers are fighting the class war "blindfolded", so to speak.

So it is up to middle class intellectuals, to "remove the blindfold", to bring the awareness of those theories, to the working class.

This is to drive home the necessity of a true Communist Party, one which calls for the Dictatorship of the Proletariat.

As the crisis in capitalism intensifies, ever more middle class people will be impoverished. They will be forced into the ranks of the proletariat. Some of them will be intellectuals. No doubt, they will bring with them the awareness of those revolutionary theories. Equally without doubt, some of them will focus on establishing a true Communist Party. It is in their best interest to do so! Self-preservation!

With a proper Communist Party, Dictatorship of the Proletariat, CP, DP, to offer direction, we are almost guaranteed a future of Scientific Socialism.

CHAPTER 14

CONCERNING SOVIET POWER

As I have previously stated, it is a fact that Soviets -or Councils, in English- first appeared, quite spontaneously, during the Russian Revolution of 1905. They were not a creation of Marxists, and could not have been created by Marxists, for the very fine reason that at that time, all of the Russian Marxists had been first thrown in prison, and were then either killed or exiled. As is well known, Lenin was exiled.

It is also well known that these first Soviets were crushed, at the same time the First Russian Revolution was crushed, in 1907. This was followed by the "counter Revolution" of 1907-14. Yet the Soviets reappeared, at the same time as the Russian revolutionary motion once again flared up, in 1914. The lesson to be learned from this, is that revolutionary motion gives rise to Soviets.

This is of exceptional importance, because as Lenin stated, "The basic question of every revolution is state power". Soviets are nothing other than *state power*! Proletarian power! A *workers' government!* A direct challenge to the authority of the capitalists!

Just as the Russian Revolution gave birth to Soviets, so too the current revolutionary motion is also giving birth to Soviets, in various parts of the world.

We know this for a fact, because in the city of Seattle, within the state of Washington, on June 8, 2020, a sector of that city declared itself to be "autonomous". They referred to this as the Capitol Hill Autonomous Zone. In the spirit of the finest tradition of the United States of America, they issued a "Declaration of Independence". No one was terribly surprised when that Declaration of Independence, was "shot down".

This self-declared "Autonomous Zone" was brief, lasting a mere three weeks, as it was crushed on July 1. Yet it gives us an idea of what to expect, after the Socialist Revolution.

A huge Black Lives Matter mural was created. There were free film screenings. Live music. A "no cop co-op" was formed. There was free food and other supplies. A community vegetable garden was constructed. Donations were taken up for the homeless. Portable toilets were set up, as well as tents and medical stations.

As well, there were frequent "town hall" meetings. The "occupants" within the Zone favored consensus decision making, although there were references to an elected Council (Soviet). The press is reluctant to make any mention of this, because the very idea of *Soviets within America,* is too terrible to print!

It is significant that the Zone embraced the "open carry of firearms". After sundown, armed guards of volunteers kept watch. For that reason, the Zone was one of the safest neighborhoods in the city of Seattle.

Those within the Zone, who were variously referred to as "occupants", or "protesters", or more accurately, "revolutionaries", initially came up with a list of three demands, although additions came later.

1. Cut the budget of the Seattle Police Department by half
2. Shift funding to community programs and services in historically Black communities
3. Ensure that protesters would not be charged with crimes

The response from onlookers varied, depending upon their class background, and upon their identification with the "Left" or the "Right".

Several of the more "kind" descriptions, from the Right, included that of the Mayor of Seattle, who stated that the Zone had a "block party" atmosphere. Others mentioned getting the impression of a "hybrid of other movements", of "part protest, part commune", a "blend of Occupy Wall Street and a college cooperative dorm", a "center of peaceful protest, free political speech, co-ops and community gardens". One of the more accurate descriptions was that of "an anti-capitalist vision of community sovereignty, without a police presence."

From this, it is clear that the Right leaning critics could not find anything "bad" to say about the Zone, so tried to come out with neutral statements.

On the other hand, the response of Donald Trump was more honest, as he spoke from the heart. He referred to those protesters, those revolutionaries, as "Ugly Anarchists"! Typical Trump! Supremely ignorant!

Of course, the occupants of the Zone were anything but anarchists, but that in no way alters the fact that they amounted to a challenge, to the authority of the capitalists! *State power!* The Zone was a challenge to the *state power* of the capitalists! The "basic question of every revolution"! No wonder the capitalists were so anxious to crush the Zone!

That in no way changes the fact that these American Councils (Soviets), one of which emerged in Seattle, represents *another government!* As yet they are very weak, well hidden, never mentioned in the mainstream press. For that matter, much of the mainstream press may not even be aware of their existence.

For the purposes of this article, I have chosen to refer to these proletarian organizations as Soviets. It remains to be seen if the American revolutionaries will continue to refer to them as Councils, or as Soviets. That is entirely up to them.

Weak they may be, *at present,* but very soon, they will become very powerful. These Soviets amount to "an organization of the workers, the embryo of a worker's government", according to Lenin. For the moment, they are no match for the "magnificent organization of the bourgeoisie". Yet in revolutionary times, "the limits of what is possible expand a thousand times", also according to Lenin! Bear in mind that we are currently living in revolutionary times!

Perhaps an example will be helpful.

Immediately after the Tsar was deposed, in March of 1917, there existed a *dual power* in Russia! No one thought this was possible! Yet it happened!

As Lenin explained: "Alongside the Provisional Government, the government of the *bourgeoisie, another government* has arisen, so far weak and incipient, but undoubtedly a government that actually exists and is growing- the Soviets of Workers and Soldiers Deputies ...It consists of the proletariat and the peasants (in soldiers' uniforms)....it is a revolutionary dictatorship, a power directly based on revolutionary seizure, on the direct initiative of the people from below, and *not on a law* enacted by a centralized state power". (italics by Lenin)

Lenin went on to stress the importance of "the only possible revolutionary government", the "Soviet of Workers', Agricultural Laborers', Peasants' and Soldiers' Deputies".

Of course, he was referring to the situation in Russia, early 1917.

Our current situation is somewhat different, more simplified. At least in North America, as well as in other parts of the world, we have very few peasants, or family farmers, as they sometimes refer to themselves. Yet the fact remains that the "only possible revolutionary government" is that of the "Soviets of Workers", along with Soviets of other groups of working people, including the military personnel, whose titles have yet to be determined.

At the time of the forthcoming revolution, the existing state apparatus, of the capitalists, must be destroyed. It must be replaced by these Revolutionary Soviets. This will be the form of the new Dictatorship of the Proletariat, a proletarian state apparatus, which will be used to crush the capitalists.

But first, the level of awareness of the working people, the common people -as that is the manner in which they refer to themselves- must be raised. The majority of working people must be won over to our side, the side of revolution, to the Dictatorship of the Proletariat.

That is where a *true* Communist Party comes into play, one which calls for the Dictatorship of the Proletariat. Only such a Party can organize country wide -or even international! - exposure of the capitalists.

As Lenin went on to state, "The class conscious workers stand for the undivided power of the Soviets...for undivided power made possible not by adventurist acts, but by *clarifying* proletarian minds, by *emancipating* them from the influence of the bourgeoisie." (italics by Lenin)

As I stated in my previous article, such a Communist Party, Dictatorship of the Proletariat, will no doubt, soon be created. We can count on the capitalists, to persuade middle class intellectuals, to form such a Party! So many of them are about to be driven into bankruptcy! Too Small to Succeed!

No doubt, there are many who are skeptical, who think that the capitalists are prepared to reward their loyal and devoted servants, those who have "given the best years of their life", in the service of their capitalist masters. Such is hardly the case!

Allow me to point out one example, one which is well known to most Americans, that of former President Richard Nixon.

Historians rate Nixon as one of the most corrupt presidents to ever held that office! That is quite an accomplishment, as the competition is so fierce! They also rate him as one of the most stupid! Also a "high bar"! But then, he is the one and only president who *wiretapped himself*!

Indeed, Nixon set up a tape recorder, in his desk, in his own office! In that office, he ordered his most trusted "associates" to commit a burglary! A burglary they "bungled"! They were caught! And the order which their boss, Richard Nixon, had issued, had been "taped"! *By Richard Nixon!* The *height of stupidity!*

Incidentally, I use the word "associates", as a reference to the people who were closest to Nixon. They were the members of his "inner circle", his most loyal, devoted followers. At least, most of them were loyal. But not all!

This simple burglary gave rise to a "public outcry", or a mass movement, to put it in scientific terms. The government officials were forced to investigate, to "find and prosecute the perpetrators, to the fullest extent of the law", to use their stilted jargon.

Nixon saw this in different terms. As far as he was concerned, the "wolves were closing in". So in the interests of "saving his own skin", self-preservation, he decided to "throw" his closest followers "under the bus". These included the people whom had committed the burglary, as well as those whom had taken part in the subsequent "cover up".

For such psychos, loyalty is a "one-way street"!

The fact that Nixon did not hesitate to "sacrifice" his most loyal, devoted followers, should serve as a warning to other servants of the capitalists! As far as the capitalists are concerned, "sentiment" is a weakness! It has no monetary value!

Of course, Nixon decided to personally destroy all "incriminating" tapes, to erase them. Except that he missed one. The one in which he directed John Dean to "stonewall" the investigation, to "bribe", to "cover up". This is commonly referred to as a "smoking gun"!

But as I previously implied, not everyone was prepared to "fall on their sword" for Nixon! John Dean was one of them! In an effort to secure a lenient sentence, he "ratted out" his former boss, Richard Nixon. The audio tape which Nixon failed to erase, supported his testimony!

As a result of this, the police were forced to believe John Dean, as opposed to their president! Dean objected to being "thrown under the bus"! Not for Richard Nixon! As a result, Nixon was in turn, forced out of office!

I use this as an example of a very powerful man, in this case a president, being "brought down", due to the revolutionary motion of the common people!

Bear in mind the words of Lenin, that during a time of revolution, "The limits of what is possible expand a thousand times"! Further bear in mind that we are experiencing a full blown revolution!

Now to return to the subject of the self-declared Capitol Hill Autonomous Zone.

Much as we admire the courage of the revolutionaries, the Soviets, of the Zone, we also have to face the fact that our Soviets are, as yet, too weak to come out with an open challenge to the capitalists. For the moment, it is perhaps best to keep a "low profile", to "bide our time", to "spread the word", to train, arm and equip those Soviets, in preparation for an insurrection.

Most working people, at least here in North America, have digital devices, and know how to use them. We would be fools not to take advantage of that fact. Further, just as Lenin focused on the Russian military, especially prisoners of war, we too should focus on all members of the military. Their military training will serve the revolution well!

I should add that Lenin focused on the Russian prisoners of war, because he was able to write directly to them. There were no military censors in the prisoner of war camps!

By contrast, there was no shortage of censors in the military! That made it impossible for Lenin to communicate with them.

We do not have that problem. We can now use the internet, avoid the printed word, and get in touch with all members of the military, bypassing the censors.

Bear in mind that common people are avid readers. They follow the news closely. They are paying strict attention to the antics of Trump, as well as others. They are well aware that Trump is facing no less than *thirty-four* felony charges. As well, other people, notably women, are alleging that he committed "more serious crimes".

The District Attorney of Manhattan has dared to do the "unthinkable", to press charges against Trump, thereby setting a precedent, "opening the floodgates", so to speak. It is very likely that other prosecutors will soon "grow a set" and "follow suit".

The results should be interesting, as so many people are paying strict attention!

Almost all common people are of the opinion that the "super rich", the billionaires, are "above the law". Their vast fortunes allow them to do anything they please! They know this from experience!

For the most part, this is true, in "ordinary times"! These are not "ordinary times"! These are *revolutionary* times! Now it remains to be seen if a billionaire, a former president, no less, finds himself in prison! The strength of the revolution is not to be underestimated!

The reason I have referred to Trump in this article, is because the mainstream press is referring to Trump, frequently and at great length! So that is what the common people are talking about! As well, they are discussing President Biden and his offspring!

It remains to be seen if the offspring, of both Trump and Biden, those who are also "in the headlines", also facing allegations of "criminal misconduct", are a true "chip off the old block", concerned only with "number one"! It is entirely possible, if "push comes to shove", that they may also "throw their dear old Dad under the bus"! It depends upon how well they have learned their lessons!

But now to return to the subject of Soviets. Without doubt, the most advanced workers have gravitated to these Soviets. That is not to say that they are class conscious. Now it is up to Marxist intellectuals, Communists, to raise their level of awareness.

With that in mind, be sure to use current events, in the interest of making a point. Stress the fact that Trump is not exceptional. On the contrary, Trump is merely a typical capitalist. He ran for president, on impulse, and the press reports that he was quite surprised, when he won. Now that he has tasted political power, it is safe to say that he wants far more.

By contrast, most members of his class of capitalists, billionaires, the bourgeoisie, are quite happy to "keep a low profile". They prefer to let their flunkies run for political office, make speeches and lie to the people. That is the only difference.

Bear in mind that time is not on our side! All of the banks are over extended, and could fail at any time! America is expected to go broke in June, unless Congress raises the debt ceiling. The various factions within Congress are at each other's throats! Each faction does not even know what it wants! Yet they are expected to come together and raise the debt ceiling! Even though they are facing financial disaster, they are focused on the next federal election!

We can expect a financial collapse, very soon. That will have the effect of dramatically increasing the level of suffering, among the common people. As their suffering is at horrendous proportions now, it may not take much to trigger a full scale revolution.

There is clearly a desperate need for "another government". That government can only be Socialist, because as Lenin said, "there is *no* other social force in the political arena, *nor can there be*"! (italics by Lenin)

Soviets! Currently "weak and incipient", no match for the "magnificent organization" of the capitalists! Yet it is these Soviets which are destined to take political power! There is no alternative!

With that in mind, feel free to flood the social media outlets, Facebook and such, with calls for the Dictatorship of the Proletariat. Make that expression a household term. Get in touch with the military enlisted personnel. Raise their level of awareness. Let them know that the government is about to collapse.

We can expect marches and demonstrations, as the financial crisis deepens, and working people are forced ever deeper into poverty. Allow the posters and placards to call for:

Scientific Socialism!

Workers of the World, Unite!

Dictatorship of the Proletariat!

CHAPTER 15

CONCERNING WHALES AND AMBERGRIS

As is well known, it is my contention that there are two huge species of animals in Okanagan Lake. These animals are commonly referred to as ''Ogopogo'', by the members of the public. The scientific community refuses to acknowledge their existence.

I maintain that one is an ichthyosaur, and the other is a whale. Both are nocturnal, so that they spend the daylight hours inside caves, as well as the winter months. Both are also omnivores, which is to say that they eat vegetation, as well as flesh. This means that during the warm months, these animals come out of the water, in order to graze.

For the purposes of this article, I am concerned with the whale, referred to as basilosaurus. The scientists consider this whale to be extinct.

The method I use, to investigate the possible characteristics of such animals, those which are thought to be extinct, is to compare them to their closest living relatives. In the case of basilosaurus, it must be similar to another toothed whale, that of the sperm whale. The two are quite similar, close to the same size and weight.

To my surprise, I found that the ''poop'' of sperm whale is considered to be supremely valuable! Possibly just as valuable as gold!

This is referred to as "ambergris", or "amber grease", or "grey amber", and according to the internet, "among the secret scatological world of whale poo traders", is considered to be the most valuable poo in the world!

Further according to the internet, this ambergris is "prized" by the perfume industry. It is "used as an ingredient in the most expensive scents". It is also occasionally used as incense, an aphrodisiac, and a medicine.

The scientists are agreed that this, the "worlds strangest natural substance", is produced in the digestive tract of sperm whales. That is about the only thing upon which they agree!

Yet as it is produced by sperm whales, could it possibly be produced by basilosaurus whales?

It is entirely possible that this ambergris is strictly characteristic of salt water whales, not fresh water whales. It may have something to do with their diet, which is different from that of fresh water whales. Or not!

There is one way to find out!

At the time they graze, they also "fertilize" the meadow. Their droppings should be examined. Bear in mind that ambergris has been described as an "elusive, smelly substance", one which is "frequently mistaken for pebbles and pumice". It may have a scent "similar to sandal wood and tobacco".

As for those who object to handling droppings, may I suggest wearing gloves. Then place the disagreeable substance in a plastic container, and have it sent to a lab.

As these animals are so huge, they very likely graze on all of the meadows adjacent to the lake, or at least, all meadows which are accessible, from the water.

On that subject, may I suggest locating a meadow which is accessible from the highway, and flying a drone around the edge of the meadow, beside the water. Look for a "slide", the place where the animals enter and exit the water. Assuming there is a tree close by, then that is a fine place for a trail camera.

There is no harm in making the attempt! According to the Internet, there is a ten-thousand-dollar reward for the person who proves the existence of "Ogopogo". That should certainly pay the expenses!

Incidentally, ichthyosaurs are distinguished by the fact that they have fins on their backs. These fins are commonly referred to as "humps". Basilosaurus has no such fin.

If nothing else, you will take part in a major scientific breakthrough! That alone should serve as sufficient motivation!

CHAPTER 16

THE ROLE OF YOUTH IN REVOLUTION

The capitalists have managed to weather the COVID-19 Virus epidemic, but are now facing an "epidemic" of bank closures.

The very few banks, which are considered "Too Big to Fail", will be propped up, with tax payer money, of course.

The remainder, which are "Too Small to Succeed", will join the countless other small businesses, as well as so many individuals, in the "shelter" of bankruptcy protection.

This is not terribly surprising, because as Lenin pointed out, in Imperialism, the Highest Stage of Capitalism, "Crises of every kind -economic crises more frequently, but not only these- in their turn increase very considerably the tendency towards concentration and monopoly".

Even the most optimistic economists are predicting massive unemployment, as well as a "Great Recession", at best.

The American national debt, which currently stands at over 31 trillion, is expected to reach 50 trillion, within ten years.

The country is further expected to "go broke" within seven weeks, unless the politicians in Washington can come to an agreement, raising the debt ceiling, yet again.

Yet those same politicians are "at each other's throats". The leaders of the two parties are not even speaking to each other. Not that either has a great deal to say, because each party is deeply divided. Different factions within each party, want different things. Yet no one seems to know just what that is!

It would appear that the one and only thing they can agree upon, is the upcoming federal election, still eighteen months away! They are focused on that election!

By contrast, the working people, the members of the public, are concerned with more mundane subjects. Such as survival!

Unemployment is widespread. Homelessness is common place. Those who are able to live in a vehicle, are considered to be "fortunate", to be" half homeless". Hunger is common place. Food banks are running out of food. Deaths from drug overdoses, are now at epidemic proportions. Mass shootings, in which four or more people are killed, are now almost a daily event. Criminal gangs now rule the neighborhoods. In the city of San Francisco, drugs are now being sold, at "open air markets". The police are powerless, in the face of criminal gangs!

Various cities are now considering calling in the National Guard, declaring martial law. And the American leaders are *focused on the next federal election!*

Without doubt, this is the very *definition* of a revolutionary situation. In such a case, as Lenin stated, the "ruling class" can "no longer rule in the old way", and the "lower classes" are "not content to live in the old way".

We have all had enough!

But as yet, there is no *true* Communist Party, one which calls for the Dictatorship of the Proletariat. Such a Communist Party is necessary, in order to give direction, to the people taking part in this revolution.

No doubt, as ever more middle class people are ruined, the intellectuals within that class, will take part in the creation of such a Communist Party. They will soon realize, that it is in their best interests to do so! Poverty is a great persuader! Those intellectuals -soon to be ruined! - have a bright future, but *only* under socialism!

After the creation of that Communist Party, it will be up to the Party members to give direction, to those taking part in the revolution.

In the meantime, Communist Party or not, we have to *prepare* for revolution, and the subsequent Dictatorship of the Proletariat. To paraphrase an old and worn out expression, "time and revolution wait for no one."

As I write this, the press is reporting that "young people", in several American cities, most notably Chicago, Detroit and San Francisco, have been "wilding". That is a word they "created", as a means of describing teens running wild, out of control, chaotic, "running amok", smashing windows and burning vehicles. But then these teens are tired of being shot, by the police, no less!

No doubt, the teens are taking action, out of a sense of deep anger and frustration. After all, they are living in poverty, and can see no way out! But only because there is no way out! Not under capitalism! Decent jobs are practically nonexistent. Even if they do manage to secure a proper education, that will get them nowhere! And they know it! They too are fed up!

This is to stress the point that the young people, in this case the teens, are no different from any other strata of the common people. They have got to be made aware of the revolutionary theories of Marx and Lenin. They are not too young to understand these theories! Their anger and hatred must be redirected and focused, on their class enemies, the capitalists!

The fact that the teens are in motion, is an indication of the strength of the revolutionary motion. It is clearly quite broad and deep.

As Lenin stated, under capitalism, it is the duty of Communists to overthrow the capitalists, the billionaires, the bourgeoisie. Our main task involves arousing *hatred*, of that *class*, among the working people. This involves raising the level of awareness, of the working class, making them aware of themselves, as a *class*, with their own *class interests!*

The young people, including the teens, comprise a particular strata of the working class. It is necessary for Communists to approach them, but in a slightly different manner, from that of most members of the working class.

Bear in mind that the young people tend to be "social media savvy", to use the expression of the journalists.

Perhaps for that reason, the younger generation has proven themselves to be excellent organizers!

Several examples may be helpful.

On February 14, 2018, a gunman walked into Margory Stoneham Douglas High School, in Parkland, Florida, and killed 17 students, wounding 17 more.

The surviving students decided that they had been used for "target practice" long enough! They responded by organizing

rallies, protests and walk outs. They also marched, "by the millions", according to the press, onto Washington, D.C., demanding gun control legislation.

A couple years earlier, in 2016, near Bismarck, North Dakota, a planned pipeline was rerouted, to pass by the Standing Rock Indian Reservation. Such a pipeline was a threat to their clean drinking water, and would destroy their sacred lands.

For that reason, Native Americans from all over the country, led by the Standing Rock Sioux, protested the pipeline.

It is significant that this protest gave birth to the International Indigenous Youth Council. Their stated goal is to "organize and empower young activists on behalf of the environment".

It is also a fact that Black Lives Matter came into existence in 2013. But then Michael Brown, an unarmed Black man, was killed in August of 2014, in Ferguson, Missouri. This gave rise to demonstrations and protests, mainly organized by young people, all across the country. At that point, BLM became a nationwide protest organization.

The point is that the younger generation has not only managed to organize, but also to establish national, and even international, networks. Excellent! Most impressive!

Now, it is the duty of Communists, to reach out to those networks, to establish connections, to give direction, to attempt to work together.

The young people of today, say that they "have no future", they have "nothing to look forward to". Even an education will not assure them of a job, because *there are no jobs! True!*

It is true that they have "no future", *under capitalism!* On the other hand, they have a "bright future", *under socialism!* Now they have to be made aware of this! After all, they are not psychics!

Under socialism, under the Dictatorship of the Proletariat, the young people will have their work cut out for them! We have plans for those youngsters! They are about to play a key role, after the revolution, in *building socialism!*

This calls for a little explanation.

After the revolution, *after* the state apparatus of the capitalists is destroyed, *after* we establish socialism, we will *still have classes!* The capitalists, the billionaires, and their devoted servants, will not just "disappear"! Nor will they "resign themselves to their fate"! They are not about to embrace their new life of manual labor! This I guarantee!

On the contrary, their hatred, their bitterness, their determination to regain their "paradise lost" will *increase tenfold!* They will resort to any lie, any deceit, any promise, any subterfuge, in an attempt to regain "that which is rightfully theirs"!

Even after they are deprived of their "ownership" of various businesses, as well as their "paper fortune", in the form of "stocks and bonds", they will still have a certain amount of wealth. This may take the form of gold or silver coins, as well as jewelry and art work, for example. Then there are the national and even international "connections" they have. This makes them a force with which to be reckoned, even under socialism!

For that reason, they must be *suppressed!* That is the reason for the *working class* state apparatus, the *Dictatorship of the Proletariat!*

The capitalists are not to be underestimated! They managed to return to power, in the Soviet Union, after the death of Stalin! They also managed to return to power, in China, after the death of Mao!

As I have covered this in other articles, there is no need to repeat it here. Suffice it to say that both Stalin and Mao were great revolutionaries. That is a fact. It is also a fact that both were human. Both made mistakes. Those mistakes allowed the capitalists, in each country, to return to power, after their deaths. We are determined to learn from those mistakes. We will *not* repeat them. The capitalists, whom we are about to overthrow, will *not* be allowed to return to power!

That is where the young people come in handy! As a key part of the new working class state apparatus, the Dictatorship of the Proletariat, they will *make sure* that the capitalists are *crushed*, wherever and whenever they try to hide!

With that in mind, I can only suggest that we "take a page from the book" of the Chinese Communists, and in particular, the Central Committee.

After the death of Stalin, in the Soviet Union, in 1953, the Russian capitalists were able to return to power. In response, the Chinese Communists took action, in an attempt to prevent a similar occurrence in China.

In particular, the Central Committee, of the Chinese Communist Party, passed a resolution, which was unprecedented. They said that the young people of China, who were protesting, should be allowed to protest! *No interference!* Except in cases of murder, arson or rape, the police and army were ordered to *stay out* of this!

This day has gone down in history as the beginning of the *Great Chinese Proletarian Cultural Revolution!* For *ten years,* the young people of China were allowed to protest, *without any police interference!*

As is well known, it is my contention that the Cultural Revolution -which was magnificent! - did not go far enough! It was largely limited to culture! It only touched on science and education!

True, the capitalists who were hiding in culture, were exposed, humiliated, reeducated and either reformed, or removed from those particular areas of culture. That is a fact.

It is also a fact that other capitalists, who were hiding in various fields of science and medicine, remained largely unaffected! They remained hidden, biding their time, waiting for the "proper opportunity" to emerge, and then attempt to seize power. That "opportunity" came upon the death of Mao!

For that reason, I can only suggest that, at the time of the revolution, on the very *day* the new proletarian government comes to power, that one of the *first* things the Central Committee should do, is issue a similar proclamation.

May I suggest the following: "The young people who have been taking part in our successful Socialist Revolution, protesting against the capitalists, should be allowed to continue with their protests. Except in cases of murder, arson, rape or looting, the police and army are ordered not to interfere."

Those young protesters, revolutionaries, should also be *encouraged* to attack their *class enemies*, the capitalists, in *all fields,* and *not just business!*

Of course, I am referring to various fields of culture and science. I use the word "science" rather loosely, so as to include such fields as education.

For that matter, I also use the word "culture" rather loosely. I rather doubt that young people consider "adult entertainment" -pornography! - to fall within the field of "culture", but perhaps that may have something to do with the gender outlook! I leave that within the capable hands of the youth!

This brings me to the subject of "professional sports". This expression, I consider to be nothing less than an oxymoron, a contradiction in terms! Sports are sports, and professionals are professionals, and "never the two shall meet", if you will excuse the terrible joke!

That which is politely referred to as "professional sports", is a business, a *big business,* and as such, is home to countless capitalists!

It is the duty of revolutionaries, Communists, to exercise *complete and total dictatorship* over the capitalists! Half measures get us nowhere! We must root them out, wherever they are hiding! Give them no rest! Feel free to show them all the compassion and mercy, that they have shown us, under capitalism! None whatsoever! That is only what they deserve! It could not "happen to a nicer bunch of people"!

That is where the young people come in! They must be "turned loose"! They must be allowed -better yet, encouraged! - to seek out and *destroy* their class enemies, the capitalists!

Yet that is *after* the revolution.

For the moment, we live under capitalism, and now we must *prepare* for the socialist revolution, and the subsequent Dictatorship of the Proletariat.

For that reason, it is now the duty of Communists, to establish contact with the young people, especially those who are protesting, taking part in the revolution, and explain this to them.

It is entirely possible that there will be an enthusiastic response.

Further, the young people who are interested, should be encouraged to establish a Young Communist League, YCL.

As Lenin explained it, "The Young Communist League must be a shock force, helping in every job and displaying initiative and enterprise. The League should be an organization enabling any worker to see that it consists of people whose teachings he perhaps does not understand, and whose teachings he may not immediately believe, but from whose practical work and activity he can see that they are really people who are showing him the right road."

It is also possible that the young people may want to form Soviets (Councils), as they are created by Revolution. That is entirely up to them.

Either way, may I suggest that, as soon as these take shape, the young people should start by explaining, to working class people, the meaning of the word Communist. After all, the capitalists have managed to persuade a great many people, that it means a "terrorist dictatorship".

Basically, it just means "common". Communist society is a society in which all things -the factories, mills, mines, railroads, airlines, shipping lines, and anything else of any considerable value- are owned *in common*, and the people work together, *in common! Teamwork!*

This is *not* to say that *after* the approaching revolution, we will live in a Communist society. We most certainly will not!

Even after the revolution, classes will continue to exist. The capitalists will be "down but not out"! They will still be a force!

We can count on them to make every effort to return to power!

This class society, immediately after the revolution, is referred to as Socialism, or the "lower stage" of Communism, according to Marx.

Under socialism, we need a state apparatus, in order to crush the resistance of the capitalists.

This state apparatus, of the working class, is known as the Dictatorship of the Proletariat. The young people, whether organized in Soviets or YCL, -or both! - will play a key role in this state apparatus, in the suppression of the capitalists.

The Dictatorship of the Proletariat will be necessary as long as classes exist.

It will be only after the capitalists are completely wiped out, that society will enter the higher stage of Communism. At that point, the Dictatorship of the Proletariat will no longer be necessary, as there will no longer be a class to suppress.

That is going to take time and patience, as under socialism, we want everyone to be useful. Indeed, many of these capitalists can be quite useful, as they have the skills required, in running a factory, for example. After all, this requires something other than manual labor!

No doubt, a certain amount of "persuasion" will be required, in order to secure their cooperation. Equally without doubt, some of them will resist, vigorously. It may be necessary to make an example of those who are most ornery! This will no doubt have the effect of making so many others "sweetly reasonable".

This is where the young people will prove to be so valuable! The young people of China proved themselves to be "great persuaders" during the Cultural Revolution, and soon, other young people, in other parts of the world, will once again, "rise to the occasion"!

This "show of force" is necessary, under the Dictatorship of the Proletariat, as long as we have classes. In due time, as all people become accustomed to working together, as a team, in the interests of the common good, there will no longer be a need for such methods. In other words, as the capitalists are gradually eradicated, the need to suppress them will also be gradually eliminated. Engels referred to this as the "withering away" of the state apparatus.

Such a society, without classes, is knows as Communism, a classless society, in which all work together, for the common good.

But first, we have to overthrow the capitalists, which requires a revolution. This, in turn, will give rise to that which we refer to as socialism, in that classes still exist, but the working class, the proletariat, will be in charge.

No doubt, a great many people are wondering, just how long can we expect this transition time, that of socialism, to last?

Lenin estimated that those of us who are over fifty, will not live to see Communism. On the other hand, he was of the opinion that "the generation of those who are fifteen will see a Communist society".

This is to say that the teen agers can expect to see the day when classes no longer exist! No more capitalists! A true Communist society!

The reasons this failed to happen, at the time of Lenin, I have covered, in a different article. There is no need to repeat it. As previously mentioned, we are determined not to repeat the mistakes of our great revolutionary ancestors. We must learn from those mistakes!

Now to return to the present moment, one of capitalism, and the duty of the young people. After all, there is no need to *wait* for the revolution! As previously mentioned, now is the time to *prepare* for revolution!

There is an urgent need to raise the level of awareness of the working class. They must become *class conscious*, aware of the existence of *classes*.

Stress, to the members of the working class, the fact that those of us who work for wages, are technically referred to as "proletarians". We sell ourselves, by the hour, for the very fine reason that we have nothing else to sell! We are wage slaves!

By contrast, those who own the factories, mills, mines, railroads, shipping lines, airlines, internet and everything else of any considerable value, are capitalists, billionaires, technically referred to as the "bourgeoisie". They make their profit, off of our labor power. They are members of a different class.

It is in the interest of the capitalists to pay us, their workers, as little as possible, in order to make as much profit as possible. It is in our interest to get paid as much as possible, in order to *survive!*

It does not take a rocket scientist to figure out that our interests are completely opposite, or "diametrically opposed", to use the technical term.

In fact, the workers and the capitalists, are *class enemies!*

Now the young people can do a great service, for the working class, by making the working class aware of that fact! As well, let workers know that revolution is necessary, as is the Dictatorship of the Proletariat. The capitalists must be overthrown, and then crushed!

There are a few other things which must be explained to working class people, as the capitalists have managed to confuse a great deal.

For one thing, the capitalists have managed to confuse the words "democracy" and "capitalism". They would have us believe that capitalism is democracy! At the same time, they would have us believe that Communism is a dictatorship! The confusion must be straightened out!

Perhaps the young people can help to explain, to the working class people, that under capitalism, democracy exists, but *only* for the capitalists! For the working class, there is *no* democracy! Capitalism is a dictatorship! Over the working class!

By contrast, socialism is a democracy, but *only* for the working class. For the capitalists, socialism, in the form of the Dictatorship of the Proletariat, is just that, a dictatorship!

The youth can further explain that our goal, the goal of Communists, is to establish a democratic republic, called socialism, for the working class. The only way we can accomplish this, is by overthrowing the capitalists, through revolution, smashing the existing state apparatus, and setting up the Dictatorship of the Proletariat. Democracy for the working class, a dictatorship for the capitalists!

It is noteworthy that the capitalists are reluctant to even use the word capitalism! They prefer the expression "private free enterprise", while referring to themselves as "entrepreneurs" or "business people". *They are capitalists!*

As all working people are well aware, the select few, the billionaires, live in the "lap of luxury". The rest of us, common people, are constantly struggling to survive. Even that is becoming ever more difficult!

The young people must stress the fact that the capitalists have to be overthrown. That requires a revolution, as no capitalist is "sweetly reasonable"! They are not at all anxious to part with their hard stolen wealth! They would sooner crawl on their bellies over broken glass!

Further stress the fact, that after the revolution, the existing state apparatus, which has been set up to crush the working class, must be smashed! It must be replaced with the Dictatorship of the Proletariat!

Feel free to use the example of so many young people being clubbed, tear gassed and even shot, by the members of that state apparatus, as an example!

After the revolution, under the Dictatorship of the Proletariat, the "shoe will be on the other foot"! The capitalists will have no rights! The former billionaires will be forced to work for a living! We will see how they like it!

For the moment, the young people have no hope, under capitalism. Rest assured, after the revolution, under socialism, they will have a bright future. We will see to that! And not just in crushing the capitalists! Training will be made available, for highly skilled jobs! Building a socialist society is going to take a great deal of work!

In summary, we can state the task of youth today:

Prepare for Revolution!

Prepare for the Dictatorship of the Proletariat!

CHAPTER 17

THE ROLE OF WOMEN IN REVOLUTION

Late April, 2023. The countdown is on. Six weeks until D Day. "Default Day". The day America Defaults on its national debts, unless the "debt ceiling" is raised. D Day may also go down in history as "Depression Day", as it is also in danger of entering a Second Great Depression!

That is the opinion of the more honest of the bourgeois economists, although they dare not mention the dreaded D word, that of Depression. Instead, they use such expressions as "economic catastrophe", "collapse of the stock market", "deep recession", "high inflation", and "high unemployment". What is that but a Depression?

Not that the leaders of the country are terribly concerned. In the finest tradition of true visionaries, they are focused on the "big picture". The presidential election of November, 2024, is a mere eighteen months away, and *that* has managed to secure their undivided attention.

Nero fiddled while Rome burned!

Indeed, President Joe Biden has just announced his candidacy for a second term in office. He is running for re-election! No surprise there.

As well, the former president, Donald Trump, has also "thrown his hat into the ring". He too wants to run for president, once again!

"*So what!*", if the country defaults!

Mind you, it is entirely possible that President Joe Biden, and Speaker of the House Kevin McCarthy, will come to some sort of an agreement, to raise the debt ceiling, yet again. No one is quite sure just what kind of agreement that could be, as there are various factions within the Republican Party of the House, and none of those factions seems to know just what they want! Yet they are not about to budge, until they get it, whatever that is!

The journalists who closely watch the political maneuvering, within the House of Representatives, have given the name of "Five Families" to the various "factions" within the Republican Party. They are speculating that perhaps Trump is "calling the shots" from "behind the scenes". His plan may be to force the country into default, blame it on Biden, and once again become president, in order to "Make America Great Again".

It may well be that Trump deserves credit for being far more cunning, than most people think!

Biden is certainly "caught between a rock and a hard place". If he agrees to their list of demands, -which are constantly changing! - he is almost guaranteed to lose the next election. If he does not agree to their demands, then the country faces default. On his "watch", no less! He will be held responsible!

The current list of demands, of the "Five Families" within the House, includes that of "remaking national energy policy, to suit the oil and coal companies, throwing the unemployed off Medicaid and food stamps, defunding the IRS and cancelling the cancellation of the student debt". For Biden to agree to those demands, would result in political suicide!

Yet even if, by some minor miracle, the two sides do come to some sort of an agreement, and avoid default on the national debt, that in no way changes the fact that the banks are grossly over extended!

According to the FDIC, there are currently "4,844 insured commercial banks" in the country. This is to say that *each* deposit, in those banks, is insured, *up to 250,000! No more!*

Yet as possibly all banks are over extended, facing bankruptcy, the FDIC has decided to support those that are "Too Big to Fail", while "throwing under the bus" those that are "Too Small to Succeed"! The "Fortunate Few" may amount to no more than five or six! Several thousand American banks are about to go broke!

The alternative is to "prop up" all banks. That only requires money! At least, *nine Trillion,* although estimates go as high as *twenty-three Trillion!*

Yet the Treasury Secretary claims that the government is not about to allow those banks to go broke. Fine! Just where do they plan to get their hands on that much money? There are only two options. Either from the tax payers, or "create it out of thin air"!

If the tax payers are "on the hook", for all those *trillions,* then the national debt will have to be raised, immediately, to *well over forty trillion!*

The alternative, to "create money out of thin air", as suggested by the Treasury Secretary, would lead to raging inflation! Far more than what we have now! This despite the fact that the Treasury Secretary *denies that this is inflationary!* She must be on drugs!

Either way, with a government default, or massive bank failures -possibly both! - the working people of the country are about to face an "economic catastrophe", to use the expression of the economists. Their suffering is about to become far more intense!

Unless, of course, the *capitalists are overthrown!* That is only possible through *revolution!* And that is where the women have a key role to play.

As Lenin stated, "There can be no socialist revolution unless very many working women take a big part in it." Yet that is most difficult, as Lenin also stated that "one of the hardest things in every country has been to stir the women into action".

May I suggest that in the case of America, a great many women have already been "stirred into action", so that the socialist revolutionary movement is now even stronger than most people think!

In the past, American women have proven themselves to be excellent organizers.

Without doubt, one of the biggest, most successful protests, which spread around the world, was the Women's March, on January 21, 2017. It took place on the day after the inauguration of President Donald Trump. It was supremely well organized!

As well, a great many women have taken part in the "Me Too" Movement, which started in October of 2017. This "prompted women from around the world to publicly share their experiences of sexual assault or harassment", according to the internet.

It is reasonable to assume that the leaders of those protests were mainly middle class, petty bourgeois. Especially as the journalists report that the Me Too Movement was started by young women, who were anxious to "break into" acting, to get a role in a movie. They found that the "price" for such a role was "sexual services" with certain very rich and powerful men, within the industry.

For many years, this has been considered to be a "reasonable request", among the entertainment industry. In fact, it is nothing other than a "polite" form of rape.

From the viewpoint of the revolutionary movement, it is most significant that the women are in motion. Further, the fact is that they may be middle class, for the moment, but likely *not for long!*

As the crisis in capitalism intensifies, the middle class will be almost completely "wiped out"! Those who have a "mere" few million "in the bank", or at least in "regional banks", are about to lose almost all! The FDIC covers only the first quarter million!

The vast majority of banks are about to "go under"! The popular understanding of "small business" is about to expand, to include those, such as regional banks, which are worth less than tens or hundreds of billions!

Those who have money in those "small, regional" banks, are about to lose them! Those who have money invested in small businesses, are about to lose that! Those who have money -capital- invested in stocks and bonds, are about to lose that! The stock market is about to "crash"! A repeat of the "crash" of 1929! *On steroids!* Welcome to monopoly capitalism! Imperialism!

That is the "one side of the coin", so to speak. The "other side of the coin", is the fact that many of the middle class people, who are about to lose their life sayings, are well educated, aware of the revolutionary theories of Marx and Lenin. After all, university education is mainly limited to the middle and upper classes. As well, it is only in university that those theories are even mentioned! And then only with a view to distorting them!

Yet no one has ever accused middle class people of being "entirely stupid". Once these people are financially ruined, they will no doubt re-examine those revolutionary theories, in a "new light".

They will face the fact that they are "ruined", and have "no future" under capitalism. On the other hand, they have a "bright future" under socialism! After the revolution, there will be a "big demand" for people who know how to run a factory! As well as numerous other enterprises, for that matter!

After all, there is a big difference between running a machine, and running a factory!

With that in mind, we can expect the intellectuals, among the "soon to be ruined" middle class, to "take the bull by the horns", and take part in the formation of a true Communist Party. After all, they will soon realize that such a true Communist Party is necessary! Only such a Party can give proper direction.

It is very likely that many of those intellectuals will be women, as so many of them are now taking a leading role in the revolution.

Perhaps it would be helpful to let them know what to expect.

After the Russian Socialist Revolution, of 1917, Lenin spoke of the role of women. He pointed out that under capitalism, "In all civilized countries, even the most advanced, women are actually no more than domesticated slaves". He went on to say that "One of the primary tasks of the Soviet Republic is to abolish all restrictions on women's rights. The Soviet government has completely abolished divorce proceedings, that source of bourgeois degradation, repression and humiliation."

Perhaps as a means of stressing the importance of this, Lenin went on to state "The status of women up to now has been compared to that of a slave; women have been tied to the home, and only socialism can save them from this".

Lenin further went on to say: "But you cannot draw the masses into politics without drawing in the women as well. For under capitalism, the female half of the human race is doubly oppressed. The working woman and the peasant woman are oppressed by capital, but over and above all that, even in the most democratic of the bourgeois republics, they remain firstly, deprived of some rights because the law does not give them equality with men; and secondly -and this is the main thing- they remain in 'household bondage', they continue to be 'household slaves', for they are overburdened with the drudgery of the most squalid, back breaking and stultifying toil in the kitchen and the family household."

Of course, after the Russian Revolution, under socialism, the law was changed, so that men and women were equal. Yet changing the law was merely the "first step".

Lenin went on to say that "The second and most important step is the abolition of the private ownership of land and factories. This and this alone opens up the way towards a complete and actual emancipation of woman, her liberation from 'household bondage', through transition from petty individual housekeeping to large scale socialized domestic services...To affect her complete emancipation and make her the equal of the man, it is necessary for the national economy to be socialized and for the women to participate in common productive labor. Then women will occupy the same position as men."

This brings us to a popular misconception. Many people, on the Left, think that under socialism, women will be expected to do the same type of work as men, to work the same hours, and produce the same amount. Such is not the case! As this subject is of such exceptional importance, I have decided to quote Lenin, at considerable length.

As Lenin explained: "Here we are not of course speaking of making women the equal of men as far as productivity of labor, the quantity of labor, the length of the working day, labor conditions, etc., are concerned; we mean that the woman should not, unlike the man, be oppressed because of her position in the family. You all know that even when women have full rights, they still remain factually down trodden because all house work is left to them. In most cases house work is the most unproductive, the most barbarous and the most arduous work a woman can do. It is exceptionally petty and does not include anything that would in any way promote the development of the woman.

"In pursuance of the socialist ideal, we want to struggle for the full implementation of socialism, and here an extensive field of labor opens up for women. We are now making serious preparations to clear the ground for the building of socialism, but the building of socialism will begin only when we have achieved the complete equality of women and when we undertake the new work together with women who have been emancipated from that petty, stultifying, unproductive work. This is a job that will take us many, many years.

"We are setting up model institutions, dining rooms and nurseries, that will emancipate women from house work...This is a matter for the women themselves...our task is to make politics available to every working woman"

In my opinion, too many people, on the Left, are focused on "demanding equality", women with men.

For one thing, such a demand requires women to work the same hours, the same labor conditions, the same productivity, and so forth. That is simply not reasonable, especially under capitalism. As most women are also responsible for house work, it merely adds to their burden!

Lenin went on to say: "It is the chief task of the working women's movement to fight for economic and social equality, and not only formal equality, for women. The chief thing is to get women to take part in socially productive labor, to liberate them from 'domestic slavery', to free them from their stupefying and humiliating subjugation to the eternal drudgery of the kitchen and the nursery."

The equality of women is possible *only* under *socialism*, and that, only after a great many years!

In the interests of the "chief task", of the "women's movement", that of fighting for "economic and social equality", to "liberate them" from the "drudgery" of "domestic slavery", may I suggest that women fight for such things as day care and nurseries.

It may help to think of these demands as part of the revolutionary movement for scientific socialism. But then, that is precisely the case!

CHAPTER 18

DEBT DEFAULT CRISIS LOOMS

The title of this chapter may seem to be rather strange, but I have deliberately chosen it, as it correctly expresses the concern of numerous journalists. Many of them are well respected, considered to be among the finest in their profession, even though "Left Leaning". Their presentations, concerning the "debt crisis", accurately states the facts. At the same time, their analysis is frequently in direct contradiction to those facts!

Yet this is characteristic, of the rather strange behavior of middle class journalists. As Lenin pointed out, middle class people, those whom are technically referred to as "petty bourgeois", are members of the most patriotic class. Their position in society leads to this patriotism! It is clearly painful for them, to even consider the possibility that their elected leaders, in Washington, would deliberately allow the country to default! They consider this to be nothing less than an act of treason!

For the sake of those who are not familiar with American politics, perhaps a little background is in order.

In American bourgeois politics, there are basically two political parties, Democrats and Republicans. The president, Joe Biden, is currently a Democrat, and the Democrats control the 100-member Senate, by the slimmest of margins.

On the other hand, the Republicans control the 435 Member House of Representatives, also by a razor thin margin, of 221-211.

This is significant, as the Republican Speaker of the House, Kevin McCarthy, can afford to "lose" only four votes, in order to get a bill passed, by the House.

Yet the American government is close to "default", which is to say that they have no money to pay their bills. They have reached their "debt ceiling". They cannot go any deeper into debt, without the approval of the House, as by law, the House controls the money.

In fact, the government "reached the debt ceiling in January", according to the economists, and has since "resorted to extraordinary measures", otherwise known as "creative book keeping", in order to pay the bills. Such book keeping is commonly referred to as fraud.

Still, the economists are pointing out that the default cannot be avoided, and may happen as soon as early June. Unless, of course, the government is allowed to "increase the debt ceiling", so that they will be allowed to borrow more money. As the House controls the money, it is up to the House to act. Or not!

So now it is up to the Speaker of the House, Kevin McCarthy, to gather enough votes, within his own Party, to raise the debt ceiling. Otherwise, he will be blamed for the American default.

With possibly a mere five weeks remaining, before the country is unable to pay its bills, it is up to Kevin McCarthy, as Speaker of the House, to come up with a bill to increase that debt ceiling. In fact, he made a supreme effort, and did just that, on April 26.

That bill is widely seen to be DOA, Dead On Arrival. It has absolutely no chance of being signed into law. Both the Senate and President Biden have vowed to kill the bill.

Some of the finest of the bourgeois journalists, who make a career of covering Washington politics, are reporting that the Republican Members of Congress are deeply divided.

In particular, they have identified no less than eight Members of Congress, whom they refer to as the "Five Families". This is their less than subtle way of comparing them to the Mobsters, of New York City.

Be that as it may, it is clear that the journalists have a very low opinion of those Members. They think that those particular Members are placing their own personal concerns above the interests of the country.

In this, the journalists are absolutely correct!

For some time, there was speculation that the Republican House Members could not possibly agree to any bill, which involved raising the debt ceiling. Yet over a period of several days, and in the process of "tense negotiations", McCarthy managed to get together just enough votes, to get such a bill passed.

The critics point out that in order to get that support, McCarthy had to make numerous concessions. Up until the moment the bill was sent to the "House Floor", to be voted on, changes were being made.

These changes are significant, as the "spending bill", that which "raises the debt ceiling", is tied in with that which is referred to as "dramatic cuts to the social safety net and its safety infrastructure".

That is putting it *politely!*

In terms of the "social safety net", it will "end critical food assistance", so that the hungry will not receive food stamps. Also, there will be dramatic cuts to Medicaid, with so many people being deprived of medical coverage. Others will have to pay a great deal more. There will be no housing assistance, for those who need it most. The number of homeless people is expected to sky rocket. The promise of President Biden, to forgive student loans, will be cancelled. Those with student loans will be forced to continue making payments. There will be cuts to early childhood education, as well as cuts to Veterans Affairs. There will be no support for that which is referred to as "Green Energy". There will be far fewer people in the IRS. In fact, it is anticipated that "countless people will lose their jobs", and not just in the IRS!

As concerns the "safety infrastructure", there will be far fewer rail safety inspections, as well as fewer air traffic controllers. Both air and rail travel are about to become far more dangerous!

Certain journalists are referring to this as a "symbolic victory for McCarthy". They are of the opinion that it will "give him leverage, in order to negotiate with Biden". Nonsense! Such is hardly the case! Negotiation is out of the question! The two are deadlocked!

McCarthy was forced to include all of those demands, in order to secure sufficient votes to get the bill through the House. If he "negotiates away" even one demand, then the Member who insisted on that demand, will change his vote, and then the revised bill will not pass the House!

On the other hand, Biden cannot possibly agree to any of those demands, because it would cost him the next presidential election! Not that the bill will ever get to his desk, because it first has to be passed by the Senate! Not about to happen! Especially as the Democrats are just as deeply divided as the Republicans!

One journalist, in particular, described this in rather dramatic terms. She is of the opinion that the Republican Members of Congress, are using the "threat" of "driving the country into default", for their own purposes, that they are "holding the American economy hostage". As she stated, now that McCarthy has finally brought the bill to the floor of the House, the "ransom demands" have finally been announced: Massive cuts to social and safety programs!

In support of this bill, a great many of the more "Right wing" economists are predicting that the "debt ceiling can be breached with only minimal impact."

In fact, that "minimal impact" would include a dramatic increase to the suffering of the "common people", the working class, the proletariat! Yet that is of no concern to the monopoly capitalists, the billionaires, the bourgeoisie!

In all fairness, we have to admit that they have a point! It all depends upon your class outlook! The members of the capitalist class, the billionaires, care not in the slightest, about the members of the working class!

Naturally, the opinion of the more honest, "Left leaning" economists, which is to the effect that "breaching the national debt", could well lead to "economic disaster", is largely ignored.

In fact, it is fast approaching! Neither Biden nor McCarthy is in any position to negotiate!

This is to stress the fact that the ruling class, in this case the monopoly capitalists, the billionaires, the bourgeoisie, have come to a state of crisis. They "can no longer rule in the old way". It is also a fact that the "lower classes", in this case the working class, and the -soon to be ruined! - middle class, are supremely well aware that they can "no longer live in the old way". This is the very definition of a "revolutionary situation", as per Lenin, in Left Wing Communism, An Infantile Disorder.

Yet that in no way changes the fact that the working class, the proletariat, is still not aware of itself as a class, with its own class interests. It is still less aware of the revolutionary theories of Marx and Lenin. Through no fault of its own, I might add. After all, those revolutionary theories are only mentioned in university.

My point is that the creation of a *true* Communist Party, one which calls for the Dictatorship of the Proletariat, is urgent. Only such a Communist Party can provide the proletariat with the *awareness,* the *direction*, which it so desperately needs.

For now, as *always,* the working class is struggling. Yet this struggle is *not focused!* How can it be focused? They are not aware that the capitalists are the enemy! They are not aware that the state apparatus must be *smashed,* and *replaced,* with the *Dictatorship of the Proletariat!* They are not *aware* of the *need* for *revolution!*

In a previous article, I compared this class struggle to two boxers, one of whom is blindfolded. Of course the capitalists are supremely class conscious, focused on squeezing as much money from the working class as possible. By contrast, the working class is not aware of itself as a class, that the capitalists are the class enemy. For that reason, the working class can be compared to the boxer who is blind folded, swinging wildly, striking out in all directions. For that reason, I say: *remove the blind fold!* Raise the level of awareness of the working class! Allow the working class to focus their anger, to strike out at their class enemies, the capitalists!

Of course that comparison is an over simplification. Yet it serves to make the point. It is absolutely necessary that the working class become *aware* of themselves as a *class, aware* of the *revolutionary* theories of Marx and Lenin, *aware* of the necessity of *smashing* the existing state apparatus, *aware* of the necessity of replacing it with the *Dictatorship of the Proletariat.* Then, and only then, can the socialist revolution be successful.

With that in mind, we can only hope that those who are taking part in this revolutionary movement, will take advantage of the internet, and either download or buy the revolutionary works of Marx and Lenin. As I have covered this in a previous article, there is no need to repeat it here.

Then perhaps a few working class intellectuals, can take part in the creation of a true Communist Party. It is very likely that a number of middle class intellectuals will join in. As their world comes "crashing down", as ever more middle class people become impoverished, the smarter ones will realize that they have "no future" under capitalism.

The revolution is bound to happen, and soon. At that point, one of two things will happen. Either the state apparatus is smashed, and replaced with the Dictatorship of the Proletariat, and we will embrace socialism. Or a different group of people will take over the current state apparatus, and set themselves up as the new rulers. More capitalism!

That choice is in the hands of the revolutionaries.

But now to return to the current situation.

It is significant that the journalists are focused on the "political infighting" which is taking place in Washington, mainly within the two parties. There is a reason for this!

As Lenin pointed out, in State and Revolution, "Take any parliamentary country, from America to Switzerland, from France to Norway and so forth -in these countries the actual work of the 'state' is done behind the scenes and is carried on by the departments, the government offices and the General Staffs. Parliament itself is given up to talk for the general purpose of fooling the 'common people'".

While the journalists are focused on the politicians, who are making speeches, the actual "work of state" is being done "behind the scenes". These speeches are nothing more than a "smoke screen", a "diversion", a "decoy", a "red herring", to put it in popular terms.

The journalists have "taken the bait", are focused on the speeches of the politicians, are speculating on the *possibility* of the *unthinkable,* a government *default*...while the people in charge, working "behind the scenes", have already decided on that default!

The fact of the matter is that "someone", who is working "behind the scenes", has been very busy, "pulling the strings" of various politicians. These politicians are mere "puppets", who "dance to his tune". He writes the speeches, and the politicians recite them!

That certain "someone", is very likely the individual who is focused on becoming president, once again. Whatever the expense! If that means sending the country into default, then so be it! He can then come to the rescue, like a knight in shining armor, riding on a white horse!

It has, very likely, already been decided, that the country will go into default, and that will result in "widespread economic devastation". President Biden will then get the blame, and the

Republican presidential nominee, Donald Trump, will easily win the next presidential election. Or so they think! That is their plan!

The journalists, in turn, are also "dancing to his tune", whether they know it or not. They are dutifully reporting on the speeches of the politicians. In this way, they too, are doing their part in "fooling the common people".

Yet it is clear that the crisis in capitalism is coming to a conclusion. Marx and Engels had a few words to say on the subject, in the Communist Manifesto: "In times when the class struggle nears the decisive hour, the process of dissolution going on within the ruling class, in fact within the whole range of old society, assumes such a violent, glaring character, that a small section of the ruling class cuts itself adrift, and joins the revolutionary class, the class that holds the future in its hands. Just as, therefore, at an earlier period, a section of the nobility went over to the bourgeoisie, so now a portion of the bourgeoisie goes over to the proletariat, and in particular, a portion of the bourgeois ideologists, who have raised themselves to the level of comprehending theoretically the historical movement as a whole."

No doubt those "bourgeois ideologist" will be a most valuable addition to the revolutionary movement, especially those who are theoreticians. Equally without doubt, they will assist the working class intellectuals in creating that which is so urgently needed, an American Communist Party, Dictatorship of the Proletariat. ACP, DP.

CHAPTER 19

PERFECT STORM OF CRISES

The COVID Pandemic. The country facing default. The banks failing. No doubt the capitalists can now understand what Shakespeare meant, when he wrote in Hamlet, "When sorrows come, they come not single spies but in battalions".

Yet the capitalists would appear to be "shouldering their burdens" rather well. Faced with financial ruin, an "economic disaster", in the form of a Second Great Depression, they have decided upon a course of action that is simplicity itself. They have decided to do absolutely nothing!

In March, Silicon Valley Bank and Signature Bank went broke. The economists are referring to this as "two of the largest bank failures in American history". A third large bank, First Republic, was "on the brink", but managed to recover. Temporarily!

Then in April, First Republic was once again "in need of financial assistance". For that reason, it was "given a capital infusion" of *$100 Billion* by other banks. The Federal Reserve gave it a $70 Billion "line of credit", and other banks donated $30 Billion. Perhaps they thought that this was sufficient to

"prop it up". Indeed, this worked, for *one whole week!*

At the end of that week, the price of a "share of stock" in that bank was selling for $3.51, down from a high of $145. As the capitalists see it, the "stocks were down 97 percent". Now the FDIC is preparing to "place it in receivership".

The lesson here, is that trying to "prop up" a bank that is failing, is like "pouring water into a dry well"! It does not do a "world of good"!

Now the capitalists are "expressing concern" that the "investors", those who "play the stock market", may be "getting jittery". They are afraid of a "panic", a "run on the banks", as those with money in those banks, attempt to draw that money out, before the bank fails. Their fears are well grounded! The banks do not have enough money to cover the deposits!

As the economists so politely state, "it is not clear that the central banks can contain the international banking crisis".

News flash! This banking crisis is not limited to America! It is international! So how can the central banks possibly contain an "international banking crisis"?

But within the country, the "central banks", the "chosen few", those which are classified as "Too Big to Fail", will not be allowed to fail! Even if they cannot "contain the crisis"! They will be supported, with tax payer money!

On the other hand, as the capitalists phrase it, "there are doubts over the viability of thousands of regional banks".

This is their stilted way of saying that "thousands of regional banks", which they consider to be "Too Small to Succeed", are about to be "thrown under the bus", about to go broke!

This is not something they advertise! Yet the Treasury Secretary, while testifying before a Congressional Committee, "let slip" that "community bank customers", those with over $250 thousand in those banks, were "not necessarily protected". Bear in mind that those deposits total *$19 Trillion!*

With that in mind, many economists, in the finest tradition of belly crawling, are assuring investors that "all is well". The banking industry is absolutely not "teetering on the brink of collapse". Although even they are forced to admit, in the interest of "covering all the bases", that the "ultimate outcome is difficult to predict".

By contrast, one of the more honest economists, has no doubts about the "ultimate outcome". He expects a "panic", a "run on the banks", a "repeat of the stock market crash of 1929". He thinks that the "coming week", the first week of May, will be "critical". He also says that, "ninety days from now, the stock market will look vastly different".

Bear in mind that this economist is by no means "Left leaning". No one has ever accused him of being a Communist! He is devoted to capitalism, right to the very core of his being. His one and only concern is with making a profit. For that reason, he has made a business of giving advice to other capitalists, concerning the best way to invest their capital.

As I write this, the journalists are reporting that they expect the FDIC to "place the First Republic Bank in receivership", on Sunday, preferably "before the Asian markets open".

In conclusion, I can only stress that which Lenin pointed out, in Imperialism, the Highest Stage of Capitalism: "Crises of every kind -economic crises more frequently, but not only these- in their turn increase very considerably the tendency towards concentration and monopoly".

Now that the capitalists are faced with a "perfect storm" of crises, and not "merely" financial, the monopolies are about to become far more complete. Thousands of "regional banks" are about to "go bust". The very few "central banks" will be left standing. Financial pillars!

Along with the "regional banks", almost all small businesses are about to "bite the dust".

Middle class people, take note! You are about to join the ranks of the proletariat! Very soon!

No doubt, the intellectuals among that class will soon become active, raising the level of awareness of the proletariat. As I have covered that in a previous article, there is no need to repeat it.

Equally without doubt, they will take part in the creation of a true Communist Party, one which calls for the Dictatorship of the Proletariat.

I mention this out of a sense of urgency. We are on the brink of depression. As well, we are also on the brink of revolution. No one can predict just when it will break out. Now it is up to us to prepare. With that in mind, may I suggest that the slogans should include:

Dictatorship of the Proletariat!

Workers of the World, Unite!

Scientific Socialism!

CHAPTER 20

TOO SMALL TO SUCCEED

On May 1, it was announced that JP Morgan Chase, a huge bank, one that is "Too Big to Fail", had just bought First Republic Bank, immediately before the stock market opened. Now the capitalists can breathe a big sigh of relief, as they have just "averted a broader financial crisis". Now that one of the "Chosen Few" has bought a "regional bank", one which collapsed because it was "Too Small to Succeed", the capitalists are convinced that they have "contained the contagion".

Fools! We can only marvel of the stupidity of such simple minded souls! They think that just because a "central bank", bought up a "regional bank", one which "failed", then that will prevent a "run" on all banks!

Common people are not entirely stupid! They are well aware that the banks have nowhere near enough money, to cover all deposits! In fact, the banks are short by somewhere between nine *and nineteen trillion dollars!* Only the first quarter million is insured!

It is just a matter of time, before that sad fact sinks into the thick skulls, of those who have considerable money in the bank. After all, there are numerous small businesses which count on having cash in the bank, in order to pay their bills, as well as make payroll. No doubt, the smarter ones will attempt to draw their money out, *before the bank's collapse!*

This is bound to give rise to an old fashioned -1929! - run on the banks! The "fortunate few", the "early birds", will be able to "grab their cash", while the "vast majority", the "Johnny come lately", will be left reciting the old refrain, "if only I'd"!

As previously mentioned, there is one lonely bourgeois economist, who is giving an honest assessment of the financial situation. This is not to say that he is principled. After all, he is a capitalist. It is simply a fact that he has found that such an approach is profitable, as so many fellow capitalists listen to him. He advises them on the best way to protect their capital, and they pay him for this.

He expects a financial collapse, as countless regional banks "go down the tubes". This will in turn lead to a Second Great Depression. He maintains that this week is "critical". He is very likely right about that.

Bear in mind that First Republic Bank had assets of *$233 Billion,* on March 31. Yet within a *month,* it was *broke!* Even with all those "assets", it was still *Too Small to Succeed!* This now famous bank, which was worth such a fortune, was still "thrown under the bus". This is to stress the fact that the middle class is being quickly wiped out!

In fact, all "small businesses" are now living on borrowed time! The monopoly capitalists, the billionaires, are about to see to that!

The monopoly capitalists plan a repeat of the Great Depression. After the "crash of 1929", the monopoly capitalists did not lose a dime! They made sure that it was the "lower classes" that paid the price!

Now with the banks about to fail, and the country facing default, the billionaires are planning, once again, to place the burden of the Second Great Depression, on those same "lower classes", the proletariat and the middle class, the petty bourgeois.

It is not just the lower strata of the middle class that will be ruined. The "upper middle class" strata will also be ruined. Those who own rather sizeable businesses, can expect to face bankruptcy. The billionaires, the members of the monopoly capitalist class of bourgeoisie, will see to that! Only the largest banks and multinational corporations will be left standing! Only those that are Too Big to Fail!

With that in mind, may I suggest, to those "upper middle class" people, that you do not have any future under capitalism. On the other hand, you have a bright future under socialism!

After the revolution, there will be an urgent need, for people who have experience, running a business. Such well respected people will be put to work, and paid accordingly.

That stands in stark contrast to the members of the bourgeoisie, the billionaires, those who do no work, under capitalism. They merely "invest" their capital, and demand a "proper rate of return", on that capital. They have no marketable skills!

Now to return to the members of the upper strata of the middle class.

No doubt, all such people are well educated, aware of the revolutionary theories of Marx and Lenin. May I suggest that it is in their best interest to take part in the formation of a true Communist Party, one which calls for the Dictatorship of the Proletariat.

There is no time to waste. That honest bourgeois economist, predicted financial devastation within ninety days. He was perhaps being optimistic.

CHAPTER 21

A SLOW MOTION TRAIN WRECK

In March and April, three banks have failed. Those banks had combined assets of close to $550 Billion. Now in May, the journalists are reporting that three other banks are "teetering on the edge", while six or eight others are "moving ever closer to default". The journalists have compared this to a "slow motion train wreck".

The economists are concerned with "contagion", in which other banks could fail, due to a "run on the banks". As almost all banks do not have sufficient cash on hand, to cover all deposits, their fears are well grounded.

Those who draw their money out first, before the banks fail, will be fortunate. The rest will lose all but a quarter million.

In order to reassure those with considerable money in the banks, the head of the Federal Reserve has just stated that "the U.S. banking system is sound and resilient." He then went on to assure one and all that there is *no danger* of any financial collapse.

It is significant that he said this with a "straight face". It is entirely possible that he practiced this speech, this *bare faced lie*, in front of a mirror. Or possibly there was no need to do so.

As Lenin stated, the capitalists "cannot act contrary to their nature". It is their nature to lie. They lie constantly. The joke among the working people, is that: "You can always tell when the capitalists are lying! Their lips are moving!"

There is certainly some truth to this. The only reason he went to such length to reassure depositors, that the banking system is stable, is because it is on the verge of collapse!

In fact, a few economists are predicting the collapse of possibly *four thousand regional banks!* Those same economists are predicting that the stock market will lose *half its value! Nonsense!*

Such starry eyed optimism! As soon as all "regional banks" collapse, and depositors lose an estimated *ten to twenty trillion dollars,* how is it that the stock market can expect to lose a *mere half of its value?* The stock market is about to lose *far more* than half!

Within a short time, only the "central banks', those that are considered to be "Too Big to Fail", will remain standing. All "regional banks", those that are considered to be "Too Small to Succeed", will "go down the tubes".

Bear in mind that the assets of one of the regional banks that just failed, was worth over *$300 billion!* Even that is "Too Small to Succeed"! Clearly, only the banks that have assets of over *$1trillion,* qualify as "Too Big to Fail"!

That which applies to banks, also applies to businesses! Any business with assets of less than *$1trillion,* can be considered to be a "small business", and as such, is *"Too Small to Succeed!"*

As the "regional banks" collapse, so too countless "small businesses" will also collapse. Those with hundreds, or even thousands of employees, will be unable to pay their work force, as those companies will have no money in the bank! *"Too Small to Succeed"!*

Workers are not about to work for free! Without a work force, all the assets in the world, will not save a business from bankruptcy! The *power* of the *proletariat!*

Within a short time, we can expect only a few, perhaps a half dozen, central banks to be left standing. They will be "propped up" with tax payer money. At the same time, we can also expect to see a very few exceptionally large businesses, multinational corporations, to be left standing.

The *extreme wealth* of the "Chosen Few", the "Monopoly Capitalists", the "Multi Billionaires", the class of people known as the "bourgeoisie", will be increased dramatically! A few of them may even achieve their lifelong goal of becoming a "trillionaire"!

The "other side of the coin", so to speak, is that of ever more wide spread unemployment, homelessness and hunger. A Second Great Depression! Far more severe than the First Great Depression!

The suffering of the common people, the working class, the proletariat, as well as the family farmers, is about to become far more intense! Further, the middle class, the petty bourgeois, is about to become wiped out! They are about to join the ranks of the proletariat!

The economists are correct, when they predict "widespread devastation"! *Unless the capitalists are stopped!*

The class struggle is about to become simplified! The petty bourgeois, the middle class, as well as the family farmers, are about to become members of the proletariat! Workers against capitalists!

As I have mentioned in previous articles, those middle class people will bring with them their awareness, of the revolutionary theories of Marx and Lenin, to the working class.

To such people, I can only stress the fact that you have no future under capitalism. You have a bright future under socialism.

With that in mind, consider the advice of Lenin, concerning the importance of a proper Communist Party: "It is only under the leadership of such a Party, that the proletariat is capable of displaying the full might of its revolutionary onslaught, and of overcoming the inevitable apathy and occasional resistance of that small minority, the labor aristocracy...only then will it be capable of displaying its full might, which, because of the very economic structure of capitalist society, is infinitely greater than its proportion of the population".

At the time that Lenin wrote this, in 1920, the proletariat in Russia was in a minority. Now in North America, the proletariat is in the vast majority. Their strength is far greater than they suspect! The only thing lacking is the proper leadership, an American Communist Party.

Lenin went on to say that: "It is the Communists Parties' principle task at the present moment to unite the scattered Communist forces, to form a single Communist Party in every country (or to reinforce or renovate the already existing Party) in order to increase tenfold the work of preparing the proletariat for the conquest of political power - political power, moreover, in the form of the Dictatorship of the Proletariat".

It is significant that at the time Lenin wrote this, the "most advanced strata of the proletariat", had embraced Soviet power, as well as the Dictatorship of the Proletariat.

Such is no longer the case. That is no cause for despair on our part. It just means that we have our work cut out for us. It also means that we have got to learn from the mistakes of our revolutionary ancestors. In this way, we can honor their memory. As I have covered this in previous articles, there is no need to repeat it here.

As for the hard core pessimists, who think that it is "no use", that "nothing will change", may I suggest that you give yourself an attitude adjustment. Or at least remain silent. Otherwise, the revolutionary forces, which are about to be unleashed, will treat you like the counter revolutionary that you are! Such an experience is guaranteed to be most unpleasant!

Under far more difficult circumstances, Lenin was able to form a Communist Party, and raise the level of awareness of all common people, the proletariat and the peasants. The same is true of other great revolutionaries. They "blazed the trail", so to speak. We have merely to follow in their footsteps, while avoiding their mistakes. Now that we have the internet, it should not be terribly difficult.

Take inspiration from the following slogans:

Workers of the World, Unite!

Scientific Socialism!

Dictatorship of the Proletariat!

CHAPTER 22

CONCERNING CLASS CONTENT

In 1920, the Soviet Union was a Socialist country, and Lenin was the first and founding head of the government. Technically his title was the Chairman of the Council of Peoples Commissars of the Soviet Union.

As head of the Soviet Union, he invited some British workers to the country, so that they might "become acquainted" with the Dictatorship of the Proletariat, under socialism, in the Soviet Union.

Those visiting workers then requested that he send a letter to the British Government. Lenin responded that it was not appropriate, but that he could, and did, send a letter to the British workers. His advice, to the British workers, is just as valid now, as when it was first written.

In his letter, Lenin mentioned that he was "not at all surprised", to find that several of his guests, working class members of the British delegation, held a standpoint "not of the working class, but of the bourgeoisie, of the exploiting class".

In particular, several of the visiting British workers, those who were under the influence of the bourgeoisie, were concerned with that which the bourgeois press referred to as a "Red Terror". The British press claimed that in Russia, there was no freedom of press or assembly. As well, certain political parties and groups were being persecuted, by the dastardly Bolsheviks. (At that time the Communists were referred to as Bolsheviks -GM)

To this, Lenin replied that the "real cause of the Terror is the British imperialists and their 'allies', who practiced and are still practicing a 'White Terror' in Finland and in Hungary, in India and in Ireland, who have been supporting Yudenich, Kolchak, Denizen, Pilsudski and Wrangel". (Those were the leaders of the Counter Revolutionary armies which were at war with the Soviet Union -GM)

Lenin went on to state that: "Our 'Red Terror' is a defense of the working class against the exploiters, the crushing of the resistance from the exploiters with whom the Socialist Revolutionaries, the Mensheviks and an insignificant number of pro Menshevik workers have sided. Freedom of the press and assembly under bourgeois democracy is freedom for the wealthy to conspire against the working people, freedom for the capitalists to bribe and buy up the press. I have explained this in newspaper articles so often that I have derived no pleasure in repeating myself."

(The Mensheviks and Socialist Revolutionaries were Counter Revolutionary political parties -GM)

He then went on to mention the names of working class leaders whom had just been arrested, including that of Sylvia Pankhurst, in Britain.

"This is the best possible reply the British Government could give to a question that the non-Communist British labor 'leaders', who are captives to bourgeois prejudices, are afraid even to ask, namely, which *class* the terror is directed against -the oppressed and exploited, or the oppressors and exploiters? Is it a question of the 'freedom' of the capitalists to rob, deceive and dupe the working people, or of the 'freedom' of the toilers from the yoke of the capitalists, the speculators and the property owners? Comrade Sylvia Pankhurst represents the interests of hundreds upon hundreds of millions of people that are oppressed by the British and other imperialists. That is why she is subjected to a White

Terror, has been deprived of liberty, etc. The labor 'leaders' who pursue a non-Communist policy are 99 percent representatives of the bourgeoisie, of its deceit, its prejudices."

That statement of Lenin, is just as true today, as it was in 1920!

The fact of the matter is that this "Red Terror", after the revolution and under socialism, is merely an expression of the Dictatorship of the Proletariat! Even after the revolution, *classes* will continue to exist, and the *capitalist class* will have to be *crushed!* Hence the "Red Terror"!

He went on to point out that there was an "old ulcer", which he referred to as the "desertion of the majority of the workers' parliamentary and trade union leaders to the side of the bourgeoisie". As a result of this "desertion" of the "working class leaders", they "entered into an alliance with the bourgeoisie, against the revolutionary struggle of the proletariat; they covered up this treachery with sentimental petty bourgeois reformism and pacifist phrases about peaceful evolution, constitutional methods, democracy, etc."

Clearly nothing has changed!

The point to be stressed is that Lenin respected the "rank and file" working people, those whom had been misled, not only by the capitalists, but also by their own labor leaders. Some of those misled workers were among the British contingent which visited the Soviet Union.

Now we have a similar situation, in that so many working people, among the "rank and file", have also been misled. They believe the lies of their own politicians and labour leaders, who speak for the capitalist class. Those working people are not at fault!

They have been deceived by the politicians and the labour leaders, those who are nothing but devoted servants of the *class* of monopoly capitalists, the billionaires, the bourgeoisie!

The astute reader may well wonder, just what the afore mentioned has to do, with the title of this chapter? The short answer is *everything!*

The fact is that Lenin *respected* the beliefs of all working people, and in response to their *legitimate* questions, drew their attention to the existence of *classes!* And to *class conflict!* So too, we must now draw the attention of working people to the existence of *classes!* As well as the *war* between the *classes!*

As working people are concerned with a possible government default, on "X-Day" -as the press has labelled it- so too we must use this crisis to raise their level of awareness. We must refer to this crisis in *class terms!*

Stress the fact that there are "negotiations" going on between the White House staff, and the staff of the Speaker of the House, Kevin McCarthy. Behind "closed doors", of course. Yet both "sides" represent the same *class! Neither side* represents the *working class!*

The "staffs" of both the White House and the Speaker of the House, are agreed that it is necessary to cut spending. They are also agreed that this must not be directed against the military. All "spending cuts" must be directed against "social safety net programs". There is no mention of *raising taxes on the billionaires!* This despite the fact that many of those billionaires *pay little or no taxes!*

The politicians justify this by saying that they do not want to "raise taxes". This statement has *no class content!* They are careful to avoid *class terms!* They are determined to *not raise taxes* on the *capitalists*!

There is a big difference between taxing the *working class*, the *proletariat*, and taxing the *capitalists*, the *billionaires*, the *bourgeoisie*!

Instead, the "negotiators" for the "two sides", the White House and the House of Representatives, are haggling over the particular "social programs" to be cut! According to the press, these cuts include "food stamps, student debt relief, renewable energy, Veterans Affairs and medicaid". The military is strictly "off limits"!

It is significant that even the military veterans, those who should be *respected* and *rewarded,* for the fact that they *served their country,* are instead being *punished!* Their benefits are to be cut!

The plan of the "negotiators" is to drastically cut the "social programs", to reduce the "safety net". This will have the effect of dramatically reducing the living standards of the working class. Ever more hunger, unemployment and homelessness, with medical services denied.

If negotiations should "fail", if the "two sides" cannot agree on the amount of additional suffering of the working class, then the country will go into "default", possibly on June 1.

In that case, all government officials agree that "priorities must be established". The *"first priority"* is to *pay the interest on the national debt!* The *capitalists must be paid!*

The economists are openly speculating on the chances that the senior citizens, those who are on fixed incomes, dependent on their old age pensions, their Social Security checks, *may be cut off!* For that matter, government workers *may not be paid!* Even the members of the military *may not be paid!*

It is clear that the economists are so far removed from reality, that they actually expect workers to continue to work, without getting paid! Not likely! Possibly the officers in the military, those who are of middle class background, may agree to this, as they tend to be so patriotic. But not the enlisted personnel! And certainly not the government workers!

Yet just as Lenin *respected* the beliefs of all working class people, so too it is up to us, to also *respect* their beliefs. Further, just as Lenin drew the attention of all working class people, to the *existence of classes,* and to *class conflict,* so too we should do the same thing!

Patience is required. After all, it is only natural to expect working people, those whom have been misled all their lives, to believe the lies of the capitalists. Especially as workers are not aware of the existence of classes! The conditions of life, of the proletariat, do not lead to that awareness!

Yet working people are not stupid! Faced with the facts, which are that *classes exist*, and that the capitalists are concerned only with themselves, then those workers can be expected to become "sweetly reasonable". *Revolutionary!* That is in their best interests!

There is no time to lose! One way or another, through government default or deep cuts to "social safety net programs", the suffering of the working people is about to become more intense!

For that reason, there is an urgent need to raise the level of awareness of the working class. Those who are aware of the revolutionary theories of Marx and Lenin, whether working class or middle class, must become active.

Feel free to use the internet. Flood social media outlets with political articles, with *class* content, with calls for revolution and the subsequent Dictatorship of the Proletariat. The capitalists have to be overthrown and then crushed!

Allow me to once again stress the importance of using the words of the capitalists, *against them!* That is certain to persuade the working people of the *existence of classes*, and of the *war between our classes!*

I can think of no better way of concluding this article, than by my usual closure. May the airways of social media, as well as the posters and banners of protests proclaim:

Scientific Socialism!

Workers of the World, Unite!

Dictatorship of the Proletariat!

CHAPTER 23

TOO BIG TO FAIL VERSUS TOO SMALL TO SUCCEED

There are currently well over four thousand banks in the United States. The vast majority of those banks, around four thousand, are classified as Community Banks. One hundred thirty-four are classified as Regional Banks, and thirty-one are classified as Large Financial Institutions, LFI. Of those LFI's, only eight are classified as Too Big to Fail. By implication, all of the other banks are classified as *Too Small to Succeed!*

Among the banks that are Too Big to Fail, the one with the *least* amount of assets is worth a "mere" $469 *billion! That* is roughly *half a trillion!* It stands to reason that any bank or corporation, which has assets of *less* than half a trillion, is considered to be *Too Small to Succeed!*

This gives a whole new meaning to the term "middle class"! By definition, the middle class is composed of people who own small businesses. Such people are referred to as "petty bourgeois", as the word petty means small, while bourgeois means capitalist. Small time capitalist.

Then there are the *monopoly* capitalists, referred to as the bourgeoisie. That is the *class* of people who own *billions,* or even *tens,* if not *hundreds* of *billions.* It is this *class,* the *bourgeoisie,* which is currently running the country.

This same *class* of people have also recently *simplified* the *class conflict!* They just made it clear that anyone who owns or controls a bank or business, with assets of less than *half a trillion,* is *middle class!* Those businesses are *Too Small to Succeed!*

We can only express our most heartfelt gratitude to the bourgeoisie, for this clarification!

This simply means that so many people, who have assets of tens or hundreds of millions, or even a billion or two (?), have just been informed that they are "middle class", "petty bourgeois", "Too Small to Succeed". As such, they are "fair game", for the bourgeoisie, the monopoly capitalists, as it is now "open season" on the middle class!

Those few, extremely rich individuals, members of the bourgeoisie, now own or control the few banks and corporations, which are classified as Too Big to Fail. They are now focused on wiping out the middle class, those who are Too Small to Succeed! In fact, those small business owners are "living on borrowed time!

Fair warning! The monopoly capitalists, the bourgeoisie, are coming after you! Your days of living the "good life", the

middle class "American dream", are about to come to an end! The class of people whom you so admire, whom you would love to join -and who can blame you? - are about to destroy you! Soon, you will join the ranks of the working class, the proletariat!

The current crisis in capitalism is about to become ever more intense! Numerous community banks, those that are "tottering on the edge", are about to collapse! The monopoly capitalists have no intention of "propping them up"! They are Too Small to Succeed!

As they collapse, this will in turn lead to a "run" on all the other banks. As those banks collapse, this will in turn, drag the middle class down with them!

Even the first quarter millions of all deposits, which is *technically* insured by the FDIC, may not be covered! After all, the FDIC recently gave *seventy billion* to First Republic Bank, in a pathetic attempt to prop up that bank. Where did they get all that money?

It is very likely that this was the money that was set aside to cover the first quarter millions of all deposits, in all the banks! "Bye bye" first quarter million which is -was! - insured by the FDIC!

We can expect a repeat of that which happened in 1929! The Great Depression! A Second Great Depression is "right around the corner"! Except that this one is expected to be far more intense!

Just as was the case in the First Great Depression, the bourgeoisie have no intention of losing any money! They have every intention of placing the burden on the "lower classes".

This is to say that the members of the middle class will soon be ruined, forced into the ranks of the working class, the proletariat.

At the time of the First Great Depression, as the stock market crashed, a great many stock brokers "took a header", jumped out of the windows of the skyscrapers in New York City, as they "lost their paper fortunes". Numerous others, middle class people one and all, found other ways to commit suicide. Senseless!

To the modern day equivalent of those unfortunate people, I can only say that there is no need to "slash your wrists".

Despair not! There is a bright future waiting for you, but *not* under capitalism! It is only *after* the revolution, *after* the bourgeoisie are *overthrown*, *after* the existing state apparatus is *smashed, after* we *crush* the bourgeoisie, *under* the *Dictatorship of the Proletariat!* That is your "bright future"!

This calls for a little explanation. Perhaps in previous articles, I have not been quite clear.

Let me start by saying that when I refer to "capitalists", I am referring to the monopoly capitalists, the bourgeoisie, those who are billionaires and multi billionaires. Such people have never done an honest day's work in their lives. They are supremely proud of this fact! Complete parasites! They merely invest their capital, and take no part in managing any business. They contribute nothing to society! For that reason, they have absolutely no skills.

That stands in stark contrast to middle class people, those who own and manage their own business, or manage the businesses of the bourgeoisie. Either way, they have skills which will be in demand, after the revolution.

I should also mention that I write in a very popular manner, even to the point of an occasional over simplification. This is deliberate. After all, during a time of revolutionary upheaval, *as we are now experiencing*, we can expect countless working class people to become politically active. Or as Lenin phrased it, in Left Wing Communism, An Infantile Disorder, "symptomatic of any genuine revolution is a rapid, tenfold and even hundredfold increase in the size of the working and oppressed masses -hitherto apathetic- who are capable of waging the political struggle".

For that reason, I have been mainly focused on the working class, the proletariat, as well as the lower strata of the middle class, the petty bourgeois. After all, many of those people were formerly working class.

That is still the case. Yet the latest developments, due to the current crisis in capitalism, has caused me to also focus on the "upper strata" of the middle class, and even the "lower strata" of the "upper class". The reason for this is that the bourgeoisie have recently "let it slip" that they plan to ruin anyone who owns or controls assets of *less than $500 billion!* Feel free to take their word for it! They are not joking!

May I suggest, to middle class people, that you first face that most unpleasant fact. I repeat, you have no future *under capitalism!* That is the "bad news", so to speak. If you will excuse the terrible joke, the "good news" is that you have a bright future, but *only* under *scientific socialism!*

Further, face the fact that scientific socialism, in the form of the Dictatorship of the Proletariat, will *not* happen by itself! Working class people -revolutionaries! - need leaders! This is to say that they need a true Communist Party, one which calls for the Dictatorship of the Proletariat. Only such a Communist Party can *raise* the level of awareness of the working class, can make them *class conscious*, aware of the *necessity* of first *overthrowing* the bourgeoisie, *smashing* the existing state apparatus, and then *crushing* those parasites, the bourgeoisie, under the Dictatorship of the Proletariat!

Such scientific socialism, which *demands* the Dictatorship of the Proletariat, is the one -and only! - true form of socialism! All other ''utopian'' forms of socialism, have proven to be an abject failure!

That is where middle class intellectuals can prove to be most useful. Bear in mind that both Marx and Engels were middle class intellectuals. As was Lenin! In fact, he was a lawyer! Scientific socialism is not just for ''workers and peasants''! It is for all members of society! Nor is it merely a ''good idea''! On the contrary, it is *inevitable!* Marx *proved* that capitalism *gives rise* to socialism!

It is simply not reasonable to expect the working class, by itself, to form a Revolutionary Communist Party, one which calls for the Dictatorship of the Proletariat. With very few exceptions, that of the occasional advanced worker -a true intellectual! - almost none of them are aware of the revolutionary theories of Marx and Lenin.

Such a task, that of forming a true CP, DP, falls upon the shoulders of middle class intellectuals. Bear in mind that working class intellectuals can assist you in this.

There is no need to wait for the banks to fail, the stock market to crash, and financial ruin, in the form of the Second Great Depression. Instead, take the ''bull by the horns'' now, and take part in the creation of a true Communist Party.

For that matter, the revolution could break out at any time. It will happen when it happens!

Yet without a proper Communist Party, at the time of the revolution, a different group of capitalists could well take over the existing state apparatus, and set themselves up as the new rulers.

Rest assured, that is precisely the plan of numerous people, those who *claim* to be Marxists, but deny the *necessity* of *smashing* the existing state apparatus, and of establishing the Dictatorship of the Proletariat! Social chauvinists, one and all!

In conclusion, I can only say that the "ball is in your court", to use a sports metaphor. Financial ruin under capitalism, or a true Communist Party, and success under scientific socialism. Your choice.

CHAPTER 24

STATEMENT IN SUPPORT OF THE 2023 FRENCH REVOLUTION

For many months, the working people of France have been protesting the plan of the French government, to raise the retirement age, from sixty-two to sixty-four. According to the bourgeois journalists, these protests have occasionally "degenerated into riots", in that the "protesters resorted to violence".

That situation changed, quite dramatically, on June 27. On that day, the French police pulled over a young motorist, for a routine traffic violation. That teen aged motorist was then shot dead.

Now the more astute members of the bourgeois press are reporting that "France is one step away from revolution". They suspect that "France has reached a tipping point", that this is "merely the tip of a global iceberg", that the French police are "overwhelmed", faced with "armed and organized migrant rioters", those who are determined to "burn and loot everything".

This statement, by the bourgeois journalists, is rather typical. It states the facts accurately, while giving an analysis which is as false as it is racist. It is also careful to avoid any *class content!*

In fact, countless vehicles have been burned. As well, numerous stores have been looted. Some of these stores have been "burned and reduced to rubble". It is true that "armed gangs are patrolling the streets", that Paris now "feels like a war zone". As some of the people who are protesting are now in possession of "military grade weapons", including automatic weapons, it is clear that this is not an exaggeration. The police are indeed "overwhelmed", as they are faced with superior firepower.

Yet to say that these same protesters are "migrant rioters", who are determined to "burn and loot everything", is pure slander.

The country is in the midst of a revolution. The working people of France, the proletariat and the peasants, along with part of the middle class, are rising up, against the ruling class, the monopoly capitalists, the bourgeoisie. That is a fact.

It is also a fact that during any revolution, criminal elements see this as merely an "opportunity". They take advantage of the "chaos", and proceed to loot and vandalize. This revolution is no exception.

In response, the French government has declared a curfew. That curfew is being widely ignored. So now they are considering the possibility of declaring martial law.

Strangely enough, the French government cannot claim that they were not warned. Two years ago, over one thousand retired military personnel, including twenty-four generals, wrote an open letter to President Macron. In that letter, they expressed their "deep concern", that the country of France was "on the brink of civil war", that "parts of the republic was given over to gangsters, Islamists and lawlessness."

It is not too surprising that this "statement of concern", as expressed by some of the most devoted servants of the French monopoly capitalists, the bourgeoisie, is also completely devoid of *class content!*

They are absolutely correct when they state that the country is "on the brink of civil war". *Class war!* Working class versus capitalist class! That is the fact which the bourgeois, and their most devoted servants, either will not -or cannot! - bring themselves to face!

Instead, they blame "gangsters, Islamists and lawlessness". Reality check, gentlemen! Capitalism gives rise to gangsters and lawlessness! As you are no doubt well aware! Yet you blame this on minorities, in an attempt to *divide* the working class, to *divert* the revolutionary motion, onto some harmless course -harmless to the bourgeoisie! - of racial conflict!

The bourgeois journalists also defend their lords and master, the monopoly capitalists, by merely parroting this racist ideology. They refer to the revolution as "riots", and hold the "immigrants", or at least those who are "from Northern Africa and the Middle East", as being responsible for this "chaos".

It is significant that even the finest of the bourgeois journalists are careful to avoid class terms! Regardless of the fact that the country is facing full scale revolution, class warfare, workers against capitalists, proletariat against bourgeoisie, they seem to be incapable of facing this fact!

This despite the fact that France has a proud history of numerous revolutions!

Yet there is at least one member of the bourgeois intelligentsia, who is able to face the truth. As he stated: "You need a popular movement, a split in the ruling class, where one portion crosses over to the revolution and offers their leadership- otherwise, it is just a riot- and you also need a crisis in the state. If all of those elements are to be fulfilled, and it leads to regime change, then we can talk about a revolution".

Although this statement suffers from a few defects, which I will not go into, as they are somewhat incidental, the intent is clear. The significance of the statement lies in the fact that the writer is considering the distinct possibility that there is "a split in the ruling class", by which he means the capitalist class, as a result of a "crisis in the state". As that is the case, he is of the opinion that a few of the capitalists may "cross over to the revolution and offer their leadership", which may lead to "regime change".

The mere fact that he mentioned this, is a strong indication that many of them, or at least the intellectuals among them, are considering this "cross over"!

Perhaps it would be helpful to compare this statement, by one of the finer bourgeois intellectuals, to the views of Marx and Engels, in the Communist Manifesto:

"In times when the class struggle nears the decisive hour, the process of dissolution going on within the ruling class, in fact within the whole range of old society, assumes such a violent, glaring character, that a small section of the ruling class cuts itself adrift, and joins the revolutionary class, the class that hold the future in its hands".

Without doubt, the situation in France has now reached a "violent, glaring character". Further, it has spread to other countries, such as Germany, Switzerland, Belgium and the United Kingdom. We are clearly "near the decisive hour"! Revolution!

Comparisons have even been made to the murder, in America, of George Floyd, and to the rise of Black Lives Matter. Not a coincidence! More revolutionary motion! Clearly, the journalists are correct when they state that the revolution is France is just the "tip of a global iceberg"!

The point to be stressed, is that the current situation is similar to that which existed immediately after the Great Russian Socialist October Revolution, of 1917. For that reason, it is perhaps best to consider the advice of Lenin, which he gave at the time of the Second Congress of the Communist International, in 1920:

"The finest representatives of the revolutionary proletariat in all capitalist countries have fully grasped the fundamental principles of ... the Dictatorship of the Proletariat and Soviet power".

Such is no longer the case! Yet that is no cause for despair on our part! We have got to face the fact that some of our finest

Communist ancestors made mistakes! They were human! It is up to us to learn from their mistakes! To paraphrase an old expression, "Any fool can learn from their own mistakes. A wise person learns from the mistakes of others!"

Now it is up to intellectuals, those who are aware of the revolutionary theories of Marx and Lenin, to bring this awareness of the "fundamental principles of the Dictatorship of the Proletariat and Soviet power" to the working people, especially the proletariat and the family farmers, as well as the lower strata of the middle class.

These "common people", as they refer to themselves, must be made aware that, at the time of the revolution, it is not enough to simply overthrow the ruling class, the monopoly capitalists, the bourgeoisie. The existing state apparatus, which has been set up to crush the working class, the proletariat, must be *smashed!* It must then be replaced by a new state apparatus, in order to crush the desperate and determined resistance of the capitalists, as they try to restore their "paradise lost". This new state apparatus is referred to as the Dictatorship of the Proletariat.

The importance of smashing the existing state apparatus, and establishing the Dictatorship of the Proletariat, cannot be over stated. If the existing state apparatus is not destroyed, a different group of people will merely take over that state apparatus, and set themselves up as the new rulers.

Incidentally, that was precisely one of the mistakes made by the workers of Paris, those whom revolted in 1871. They established the first socialist republic, and referred to it as the Paris Commune. Yet they failed to smash the existing state apparatus! A huge mistake!

To the modern day revolutionaries of France, I can only say: Honor your heroic ancestors, the Communards, by following in their footsteps, while not repeating their mistakes! Learn from their mistakes! At the time of the next French Revolution, smash the existing state apparatus, and replace it with a new state apparatus, the Dictatorship of the Proletariat!

This brings us to Soviet power.

Almost all revolutions give birth to a proletarian creation, an organization called a Soviet, or Council, in English, or Sovietique, in French. As the revolution gains strength, these Soviets become ever more powerful.

In Russia, at the time of the February Revolution of 1917, the Soviets were almost as powerful as the Russian government, under Kerensky. In fact, the Soviets were so powerful, that the government agents were afraid to arrest Lenin, at the time he returned from exile in April, of that year.

Now it is up to conscious people, those who are aware of the scientific theories of Marx and Lenin, Communists, to bring to the working class the awareness of those theories.

At that same International, Lenin went on to state the tasks laid out for us. As it is too important, I have decided to quote it at length:

"The victory of socialism (as the first stage of communism) over capitalism requires that the proletariat, as the only really revolutionary class, shall accomplish the following three tasks. First -overthrow the exploiters, and first and foremost the bourgeoisie, as their principle economic and political representative; utterly rout them; crush their resistance; absolutely preclude any attempt on their part to restore the yoke of capital and wage-slavery. Second- win over and bring under the leadership of the Communist Party, the revolutionary vanguard of the proletariat, not only the entire proletariat, or its vast majority, but all who labor and are exploited by capital; educate, organize, train and discipline them in the actual course of a supremely bold and ruthlessly firm struggle against the exploiters; wrest this vast majority of the population in all the capitalist countries from dependence on the bourgeoisie; imbue it, through its own practical experience, with confidence in the leading role of the proletariat and of its revolutionary vanguard. Third- neutralize, or render harmless, the inevitable vacillation between the bourgeoisie and the proletariat, between bourgeois democracy and Soviet power, to be seen in the class of petty proprietors in agriculture, industry and commerce - a class which is still fairly numerous in nearly all advanced countries, although comprising only a minority of the population- as well as in the stratum of intellectuals, salary owners, etc., which correspond to this class."

Without doubt, that is indeed a "tall order"! Equally without doubt, that is clearly beyond the ability of an individual, or a number of individuals working separately. An organization is required, a gathering of intellectuals, conscious people, Communists, with a common goal. Of course, such an organization is referred to as a Communist Party. The only true Communist Party is one which calls for the Dictatorship of the Proletariat, the "touchstone of a true Marxist", according to Lenin.

Now that we have the internet, the task of raising the level of awareness of the working people is much easier than it was, many years ago. The vast majority of workers are now cultured, complete with access to various digital devices. Instead of passing out leaflets, we can now send emails!

Further, it is most encouraging that key works of Lenin, such as State and Revolution, and Left Wing Communism, An Infantile Disorder, are now available in audio form. They can be downloaded from the internet. This is most useful, as a person can listen to those revolutionary writings of Lenin, perhaps while driving, running a machine, doing house work, or simply relaxing at home.

The fact that conscious people have gone to the trouble of making these works of Lenin available, in audio form, is an indication of the strength of the revolutionary motion.

Now it is of vital importance to form a true Communist Party, Dictatorship of the Proletariat, in all countries, and not just

France. The French are currently leading the revolution, which is spreading to western Europe and possibly beyond.

It is very likely only after the revolution is successful in France, and at least several other highly industrialized countries, that we can form a true International Communist Party.

By and large, it is only middle class intellectuals who are aware of the revolutionary theories of Marx and Lenin. For that reason, the onus is on them to form a true Communist Party, perhaps with the assistance of working class intellectuals.

Be discreet! Use the internet! Do not use the telephone! All such conversations are monitored! Do not meet in person! Do not make it easy for the government agencies! Be vocal but anonymous!

It is only a matter of time -probably a short time! - before the working people become class conscious. No doubt powerful Soviets will also be created. These Soviets will then challenge the existing bourgeois governments for state power. Only then will it be safe for true Communist Parties to go public.

At that point, Lenin let us know what to expect.

In 1920, at the Second Congress of the Communist International, Lenin stated that:

"World imperialism shall fall when the revolutionary onslaught of the exploited and oppressed workers in each country, overcoming resistance from petty bourgeois elements and the influence of the small upper crust of labor aristocrats, merges with the revolutionary onslaught of hundreds of millions of people who have hitherto stood beyond the pale of history, and have been regarded merely as the object of history".

With that in mind, consider the fact that we are very close to that point. This is bound to give rise to that which Lenin foresaw:

"If our comrades in all lands help us now to organize a united army, no shortcomings will prevent us from accomplishing our task. That task is the world proletariat revolution, the creation of a world Soviet republic."